MARRIAGES
of
ORANGE COUNTY
VIRGINIA
1747–1810

COMPILED AND PUBLISHED
by
CATHERINE LINDSAY KNORR

Please direct all correspondence and orders to:

www.southernhistoricalpress.com
or
SOUTHERN HISTORICAL PRESS, Inc.
PO BOX 1267
375 West Broad Street
Greenville, SC   29601
southernhistoricalpress@gmail.com

ISBN #0-89308-252-X

Printed in the United States of America

To

Hermie

"the mos' bes' nice man in all the world."

YORK, 1634, ORIGINAL SHIRE

NORTHUMBERLAND, 1648

LANCASTER, 1651   WESTMORELAND, 1653

RAPPAHANNOCH   MIDDLESEX   STAFFORD, 1664
1656 - 1692   1673
                                      PRINCE WILLIAM, 1731

ESSEX   RICHMOND   FAIRFAX, 1742
1692   1692

                KING GEORGE
                   1721

CAROLINE   SPOTSYLVANIA
1728   1721

            ORANGE, 1734

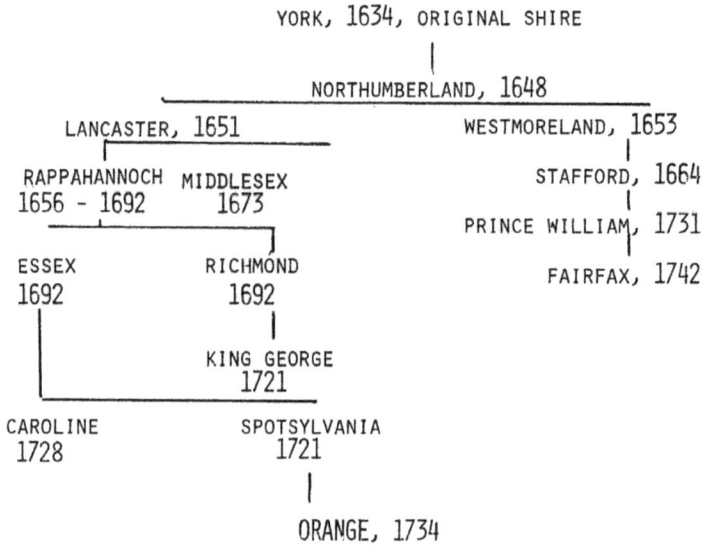

ROBINSON'S VIRGINIA COUNTIES, CHART 9, PAGE 168

Culpeper

Madison

Stafford

Greene

Orange

ORANGE

Spotsylvania

Albemarle

Louisa

Publisher's Preface

Mrs. Knorr died in 1975, and after her death these books of marriage records were kept in print and sold by her late husband. Upon his death, they became the property of her grandson, Hal Wyche Greer, III, of Marietta, Georgia, who continued to sell them on a limited basis.

In mid-1981 I sought to find Mr. Greer to discuss with him the possibility of obtaining the exclusive publishing and sales rights to these 14 titles. In due time, Mr. Greer and I were able to negotiate a contract for my exclusive sales and publication rights to these books. It was agreed that Mr. Greer would have a final voice on the changing of the format of any of these titles when they needed to be reprinted. I suggested to Mr. Greer that when these various books sold out and a reprinting had to be done, that for the sake of cost, I would publish them in a 6" x 9" page size, but that the format and style would remain the same, and this was agreed upon.

The reader is cautioned to note that these new 6 x 9 pages are typed verbatum from Mrs. Knorr's original copy, and page by page, so that new indexing was not required. It was also decided that when a book went out of print, it would be retyped on an electric typewriter with a carbon ribbon for better legibility. As publisher, I felt it was important to call to the attention of the reader these changes and the reason for eventually bringing out all of these titles in a 6 x 9 book.

The Rev. S. Emmett Lucas, Jr.
Publisher

PREFACE

For the thirteenth time thousands of persons interested in genealogy
and history are indebted to Catherine Lindsay Knorr for her compilations
of marriage bonds and ministers' returns for various Virginia counties.
Through her labors we now have the Marriages of Orange County 1747-1810.

The present volume is perhpas the most difficult Mrs. Knorr has
undertaken to compile. There is no contemporary marriage register of
Orange County, however there is in the Clerk's Office a XX Century
arrangement of the marriages which was compiled some years ago from the
marriage bonds, ministers' returns, a list of marriages in the back of
Deed Book #17, and other records. It was discovered, however, that this
arrangement was not trustworthy as there were many errors and omissions
of every description. In preparing her present work, Mrs. Knorr is
indebted to the Honorable Henry C. DeJarnette, Clerk of the Circuit
Court of Orange County, for the courtesy extended by him in allowing her
access to the original marriage bonds and ministers' returns each of
which was carefully inspected and all information of genealogical
import is given herein.

With patience and care these small pieces of paper, often broken
in the folds and crumbling, were minutely examined. It was not unusual
to find the orthography of the proper names a challenge and it was noted
that the same name often appears variously spelt in the same document.
Thus we may find the following names, for example spelled interchangeably:
Acree and Acry; Ahart, Aheart, Ayheart and Ehart; Burras, Burrus,
Burroughs and Burrows; Chissam, Chism, Chishalm; Fleak, Fleck and Fleek;
Gaar, Gaer, Gear and Geer; Pain, Paine, Payn and Payne; Pettus, Pettis,
Pettess and Pettys. The signatures of the bridegroom, securities, and
witnesses on these marriage bonds and accompanying consents were often-
times difficult to decipher. It was also noted that the marriage
register in the Clerk's Office has been altered to suit the fancy of
some searchers: for example the surname Camp has been altered to Champ
and other unauthorized alterations attempted.

Mrs. Knorr discovered that the entire bundle of marriage bonds for
1787 was missing from the files and an intensive search failed to locate
them. It was thus impossible to check the marriages for this year and
they are given in this volume as they appear in the Marriage Register
before mentioned as they were in their proper file in the Clerk's Office
when it was compiled.

Orange County was formed from Spotsylvania County in 1734 and com-
prised a vast area on both sides of the Blue Ridge Mountains out of which
has subsequently been formed more than three dozen counties in Virginia
alone. It was named for William Prince of Orange in Holland, who became
King William III of England. Although King and Queen County had been named

for King William and his Queen in 1691 shortly after they ascended the English throne and King William County had been named for him the year of his death (1702), it is said the Honorable Alexander Spotswood (1676-1740), who was Governor of Virginia 1710-1722, was instrumental in having the new county named Orange having a great fondness for King William III under whom he held a commission as an officer in the English Army. At the time of the formation of Orange County from Spotsylvania County (which has been named for Governor Spotswood upon its formation in 1721) he was the leading citizen of upper Spotsylvania County.

The first settlement of white men in the area now embraced in Orange County was the result of the enterprise of Governor Alexander Spotswood who brought over in 1714 a group of German artisans to work in the iron mines and furnace which he established on the Rappahannock River. These origianl settlers, a group of twelve families, who soon migrated to Fauquier County, were followed by other Germans in 1717 and 1719 who established themselves at Germanna in a bend of the Rapidan River near its junction with the Rappahannock River. This group moved into present day Madison County about 1726 while their benefactor was in England.

After 1720 the colonization of the region to later become Orange County was steady and the original German settlers were rapidly joined by settlers of English, Scotch and Irish extraction both from their native countries and by migration from tidewater Virginia. These people were joined by others from New Jersey, Pennsylvania and elsewhere and settlers in great numbers came over the mountains and down the Shenandoah Valley into Frederick County (which was formed from Orange County in 1743) and Agusta County (which was formed from Orange County in 1745).

After a sojourn in England (where he was married in 1724/5 to Anne Butler Brayne), Governor Spotswood returned to Virginia about 1730 and established himself at Germanna and engaged in the iron industry. Here Colonel William Byrd of "Westover" on the James River visited him in September 1732 at his "enchanted Castle" and has left us a most interesting account of his visit in his essay, A Progress to the Mines. Germanna was the home of Colonel Spotswood until his death in 1740. His last will and testament was handsomely restored and beautifully set in a protective panel in the Clerk's Office in 1938 by The Golden Horseshoe Chapter, National Society, Daughters of the American Revolution. These same ladies at the same time and in like manner also exhibited the last will and testament of James Madison (1751-1836), fourth President of the United States, who, though born at his maternal grandmother's in King George County, was raised from earliest infancy in Orange County it being the home of his parents Colonel and Mrs. James Madison. President Madison died and is buried at this handsome residence "Montpelier" about ten miles east of Orange Courthouse. Orange County was also the birthplace of the twelfth president of the United States, General Zachary Taylor (1784-1850), who was a cousin of James Madison, both being the great-grandchildren of James Taylor, Gentleman, (1675-1729), of King and Queen County, Virginia.

The first recordings of the new county of Orange are interesting and give us an insight into the procedure and those connected with it:

ORANGE COUNTY

Be it remembered that on the twenty first day of January in the year 1734.

A Commission of the Peace directed to Augustine Smith, Goodrich Lightfoot, John Taliaferro, Thomas Chew, Robert Slaughter, Abraham Field, Robert Green, James Barber, John Finlason, Richard Mauldin, Samuel Ball, Francis Slaughter, Zachary Taylor, John Lightfoot, James Pollard, Robert Eastham, Benjamin Cave, Charles Curtis, Joist Hite, Morgan Morgan, Benjamin Borden, John Smith, George Hobson and a dedimus for administering the oaths &c. to the said Justices being read the said John Finlason and Samuel Ball pursuant to the said dedimus adminstered the oaths appointed by Act of Parliament to be taken instead of the Oaths of Allegiance and Supremacy the oath appointed to be taken by an Act of Parliament made the first year of the Reign of his late Majesty King George the first, entituled an Act for the further security of his Majesties person and Government and the succession of the Crown in the heirs of the late Princess Sophia being Protestants and for extinguishing the hopes of the pretended Prince of Wales and his open and secret abettors, unto Augustine Smith and John Taliaferro who severally subscribed the test and then the said John Finalson and Samuel Ball administered the oaths of a Justice of the Peace of a Justice of the County Court in Chancery unto the said Augustine Smith and John Taliaferro and afterwards the said Augustine Smith and John Taliaferro pursuant to the said dedimus administered all and every of the said oaths unto Thomas Chew, Robert Slaughter, Abraham Field, Robert Green, James Barber, John Finlason, Samuel Ball, Francis Slaughter, John Lightfoot, James Pollard and Benjamin Cave who severally subscribed the test.

The record proceeds with the following appointments: Clerk of the Court, Henry Willis, Gentleman; Sheriff, Benjamin Cave, Gentleman; Under-Sheriff, William Henderson; Surveyor, James Wood, Gentleman; and King's Attorney, John Mercer, Gentleman. The surveyors of the highways in their several precincts were next named, viz: Jonas Jenkins, Alexander McQueen, John Landrum, John Read, Charles Dewit, Jr., Henry Field, George Wheatley, Edward Abbot, Christopher Zimmerman, Michael Clore, John Howard, James Barber, Robert Cave, John Garth, Thomas Jackson, Anthony Head, Alexander Waugh, Benjamin Porter, John Marks, Edward Haly, William Smith, James Coward, John Snow, Charles Stephens, and Edward Franklin.

I think that the manner in which the justices made arrangements with Colonel Alexander Spotswood is interesting, and I quote verbatim:

ORANGE COUNTY

In Complyance to an Order of Court dated the 21st day of January 1734, We the subscribers went to Colonel Spotswood to know upon what terms he would let his land for a Ferry at Germanna, and his Honor was pleased to say that he would let the plantation at the Ferry together with land sufficient for two hands to work for the term of seven years for six hundred and thirty pounds of tobacco per year but debars the keeping of a tipling house or hoggs running at large at the Ferry plantation and further more sayeth not.

Robert Slaughter
Abraham Field
Robert Green

Ordered that the Honorable Colonel Spotswood's Letter in Relation to placeing the Courthouse be recorded.

Whereas I have been desired to declare upon what terms I will admitt the Courthouse of Orange County to be built upon my land in case the Commissioners for placing the same should judge the most convenient situation thereof to be within the bounds of my Patent, And for as much as I am not only willing to satisfy such Commissioners that no obstruction in that point will arise on my part, but am also disposed to make those terms as easie to the County as can well be expected; I do therefore hereby declare that I consent to the building a Courthouse, prison, pillory and stocks, on any part of my lands not already leased or appropriated. And that I will convey in the form and manner which the Justices of the County can in reason require, such a quantity of land as may be sufficient for setting the said Buildings on, with a convenient court yard thereto, for the yearly acknowledgement of one pound of Tobacco, And more over that I will allow to be taken gratis off my land all the timber or stone which shall be wanted for erecting and repairing the said buildings.

Given under my hand at Germana the 6th day of January 1734/5.

A. Spotswood

As before mentioned Frederick County was formed from Orange County in 1743 and in 1745 Augusta was formed. In 1749 the land north of the Rapidan River was cut off to form Culpeper County which in turn was the parent of Madison in 1793 and Rappahannock County in 1833. In 1838 Orange County again yielded a portion of its territory to form Greene County.

While Mrs. Knorr makes reference to one marriage contract of 1747 it will be noted that the recorded marriages begin a few years later as those found in deed books and fee books begin 1757. The earliest marriage bonds begin in 1775 and as there may be those who consult this

book who may not be familiar with the legal form of such document I wish
to quote one verbatim:

Know all men by these presents that we William Strother and William
Cave of Orange County are held and firmly bound unto our Sovereign
Lord King George the Third by the Grace of God King of Great Brittain,
France, & Ireland, Defender of the Faith &c. in the full sum of Fifty
Pounds Current Money to be paid to the said Lord the King his heirs
and successors to which payment well and truly to be made we bind
ourselves our heirs executors and administrators jointly and severly
firmly by these presents sealed with our seals and dated this 9th day
of June 1775.
Whereas there is a marriage suddently intended to be solomnized between the above bound William Strother and Ann Kavenah, widow, the
condition of the present obligation is such that if there is no lawful
cause to obstruct the same then this obligation to be void else to
remain in full force.

Sealed and Delivered in   William Strother (Seal)
the present of Fra.^{s} Taylor   William Cave   (Seal)

The above bond is endorsed on the reverse:
                    Wm Strothers
                    Marriage Bond
                    June 9, 1775

Again, we salute Mrs. Knorr as she places her thirteenth volume in
our hands.

                                    George H. S. King

Fredericksburg, Virginia
November 11, 1959

5 October 1777. John ABEL and Margaret Tinder. Found in Deed Book 17. Both of St. Thomas' Parish. Notation: by Banns. p 6

30 July 1805. John S. ABELL and Sally King. "Consent of father" not named. Sur. Caleb Abell. Wit. Joseph Hilman, Sr., Moses Bledsoe and Richard Rhoades. p 66

20 November 1804. Francis ABRAHAM and Jestin Mallory. Sur. Thomas Proctor. Married 21 November by Rev. Robert Jones. p 64

21 December 1798. James ACRE and Elizabeth Acre, spinster. Sur. John Morris. p 47

24 December 1804. William ACREE and Rebecca Morris. Sur. John Morris, who makes oath William is over 21. Married by Rev. Hamilton Goss. p 65

7 April 1781. Benjamin ADAMS and Nelly Coleman. Sur. Lawrence Egbert. Both of St. Thomas' Parish. Register says 1780 and Milly; bond says 1781 and Nelly. p 10

16 May 1782. James ADAMS and Mary Chambers, dau. Thomas Chambers, who consents. Sur. George Bledsoe. Wit. William Adams. Both of St. Thomas' Parish. p 11

22 December 1795. Elisha ADAMS and Delia Smith, dau. James Smith, who consents. Sur. John Adams. p 38

17 May 1810. James ADAMS and Patsey Harper, who writes her own consent. Sur. Ellick Hawkins. Wit. Benjamin Sanders, James Jones and William Perry. p 78

20 June 1807. Thomas B. ADAMS and Judith Burnley, dau. Frances Burnley, who consents. Sur. William B. Taylor. Wit. Charles Bell. Married by Rev. Robert Jones. p 71

3 May 1773. James ADDAMS and Eley Welch. Found in Deed Book 17. Both of St. Thomas' Parish. p 203

17 November 1808. George AERY and Elizabeth Shifflet. Married by Rev. George Bingham. p 73

25 March 1793. Abram AHART, Jr. and Judith Kirk, who writes her own consent. Sur. George McDaniel. Wit. John Wayland. Abram, son of Abram Ahart, Sr. who consents for him. p 32

21 September 1777. Jacob AHART and Mary Bruce. Both of St. Thomas' Parish. Found in Deed Book 17 by J. W. Browning. Notation: by Banns. p 6

1

12 December 1783. John AHART and Peggy Pearson, dau. Robert Pearson. Sur. Galin White. Wit. John White. In St. Thomas' Parish. p 13

16 August 1788. William AIRY and Mary Stowers. Writes her own consent. Sur. Lewis Stowers. Wit. James Taylor. p 22

13 January 1786. Robert ALCOCK and Mary Bell, widow. Sur. James Taylor. p 18

15 March 1785. William ALCOCK and Catey Bell. Sur. James Taylor. Wit. Robert Alcock. p 15

10 April 1776. James ALEXANDER and Jerusa Townsend. Found in Deed Book 17. Both of St. Thomas' Parish. Notation: by Banns. p 6

14 June 1792. James ALEXANDER and Franky Ahart. Married by Rev. George Eve. p 30

23 September 1787. James ALLEN and Patsy Woolfolk. Sur. Thomas Woolfolk, Jr. p 20

22 December 1808. John ALLEN and Sarah Head. Married by Rev. Jacob Watts. p 74

12 August 1801. William ALLEN and Elizabeth Wallace, dau. James Wallace, who consents and is surety. Married 13 August but minister's name torn off. p 54

19 October 1798. Henry ALVIS and Agnes Armstrong. Married by Rev. George Bingham. p 46

18 April 1798. Joseph AMOS and Ann Marr, spinster. Sur. Alexander Marr. p 46

26 February 1796. Benjamin AMUS and Nancy Acre. Sur. William Acre. Wit. James Taylor, Jr. p 39

28 December 1801. Henry ANGELL and Nancy Beazley. Sur. Richard Williams. Married 31 December by Rev. Hamilton Goss. p 55

27 August 1804. Robert ANCELL and Frances Pereson. Sur. Thomas Cox, who makes oath both are over 21. Married by Rev. George Bingham. p 64

14 October 1806. Benjamin ANDERSON and Mary Miller, dau. John Miller who consents and is surety. He also makes oath Benjamin is over 21. Married by Rev. George Bingham. p 69

30 May 1805. Joel ANDERSON and Lucy Reddish. Married by Rev. George Bingham. p 66

24 October 1798. Nathan D. ANDERSON and Milley Bell. Sur. Thomas Bell.
p 47

22 May 1809. William ANDERSON and Lucy Hawkins, dau. Reubin Hawkins, who
consents. Sur. Benjamin Sanders. Wit. Roddy Hawkins and James
Hawkins. Married 25 May by Rev. Jeremiah Chandler. p 75

21 December 1773. Jacob ARHART and Nanny Ballard. Found in Deed Book
17. Both of St. Thomas' Parish. p 203

9 September 1809. William B. ARNALL and Jane Martin, dau. William H.
Martin, who consents and is surety. Married 10 September by Rev.
Robert Jones. p 76

8 February 1789. James ARNOLD and Elizabeth Atkins, spinster. Sur.
James Atkins. Wit. James Taylor. p 25

27 January 1802. Thomas ARNOLD and Peggy Sanford. Sur. Pierce Sanford.
Married 28 January by Rev. Robert Jones. p 56

23 July 1804. Willis ARNOLD and Margaret Golden. Sur. Julien King,
who makes oath Margaret is over 21. p 63

25 January 1780. Edward ATKINS and Frankie Wisdom. Both of St. Thomas'
Parish. Sur. Joseph Atkins. p 9

24 December 1801. Gentre ATKINS and Frankey Chiles. Sur. Wisdom Atkins.
Nancy Atkins consents for Gentre. p 55

23 November 1788. Hezekiah ATKINS and Sally Chiles, who writes her own
consent. Sur. James Chiles. Wit. Dillard Collins and Henry Chiles.
p 23

29 April 1777. James ATKINS and Anny Pigg. Found in Deed Book 17.
Both of St. Thomas' Parish. Notation: by Banns. p 5

6 April 1792. James ATKINS and Elizabeth Poe. Sur. John Smith. Wit.
James Taylor. p 30

22 November 1803. James ATKINS, Jr. and Fanny Atkins. James Atkins
consents for Fanny; no relationship stated. Sur. Wisdom Atkins.
Wit. John Atkins. p 61

9 February 1778. John ATKINS and Anne Burrass, dau. Edmund Burrass,
who consents. Sur. Joseph Atkins. Wit. Thomas Rucker and Thomas
Wisdom. p 7

20 December 1806. John ATKINS and Peggy Campbell. William Tatum of
Albemarle, guardian of Peggy, consents for her and is surety. p 69

22 September 1775. Joseph ATKINS and Milly James. Found in Deed Book
17. Both in St. Thomas' Parish. Notation: by Banns. p 4

9 January 1787. Joseph ATKINS and Ann Atkins. Sur. John Atkins, Jr.
p 19

7 June 1797. Mallachi ATKINS and Sally Mountacue, who gives her own
consent. Sur. Roger Bell. Wit. John Anderson and Franky Anderson.
p 43

1 March 1786. Silence ATKINS and Frances Jennings, dau. John Jennings,
who consents. Sur. Luke Jennings. Wit. Lidde Jennings. p 18

16 January 1803. Waller ATKINS and Sally Atkins. Sur. James Morton,
who makes oath both are over 21. p 59

4 February 1777. William ATKINS and Wintifred Briant. Found in
Deed Book 17. Both of St. Thomas' Parish. Notation: by Banns. p 5

24 September 1800. Wisdom ATKINS and Nancy Atkins. Sur. Edward Atkins,
who makes oath Nancy is 21 years of age. Wit. Charles Bell and
George C. Taylor. p 52

19 January 1802. Thomas ATKINSON and Sally Sylvie, dau. Sarah Silby,
who consents. Sur. Bernard Atkinson. Wit. Solly Atkinson. Signed
Barrett Atkinson. p 56

27 February 1775. Robert AUSBUM and Milly Cudden. Found in Deed Book
17. Both of St. Thomas' Parish. Notation: by Banns. p 3

22 December 1810. David AUSTIN and Fanny Williams, dau. John Williams,
who consents. Sur. James Beazley. Wit. George Bingham, Eli and
Nancy Austin and Joseph Williams. David is of Albemarle County and
son of Nancy Austin, who consents. Married 27 December by Rev. Jacob
Watts. p 79

24 December 1807. John AUSTIN and Gestina Burrus. Married by Rev.
George Bingham. p 72

25 December 1804. Richard AUSTIN and Mary Snow. Married by Rev. George
Bingham. p 65

17 -   1782. Robert BARBER and Nancy Spradling, dau. David Spradling,
who consents. Wit. William Barton and John Dents. This is consent
only addressed to James Taylor, Clerk. p 11

- -   1790. Robert BARBER and Nancy Spradling, dau. David Spradling,
who consents. Wit. William Barton and John Dent. This bond is
undated but in the 1790 package. no page

9 June 1797. Robert BARBER and Nancy Spradling, spinster. Sur. William
Barton. Wit. James Taylor. All three of the above records are in
Orange County; all evidently the same marriage. p 43

14 October 1807. Joseph BAILES and Cency Olliver, dau. Frances Olliver, who consents. Sur. Daniel Olliver. Wit. Hopeful Wood. Married 16 October by Rev. Jacob Watts. p 71

18 November 1801. Lewis BAILEY and Lucy Mallory. Married by Rev. George Bingham. p 55

28 October 1800. William P. BAILEY and Mary L. Grymes, 21 years of age. Sur. Garnett Peyton. Wit. Reynolds Chapman. p 52

2 June 1805. James BAILY and Nancy Mallory. Married by Rev. George Bingham. p 66

13 January 1786. Larkin BALLARD and Elizabeth Gaines, dau. Sally Gaines, who consents. Sur. Curtis Ballard. Wit. Thomas Watts. p 18

25 December 1797. Medley BALLARD and Jane Dehoney, dau. Thomas and Hanner Dehoney, who consent. Sur. Uriah Anderson. p 44

8 March 1778. Thomas BALLARD and Elizabeth Smith. Found in Deed Book 17. Both of St. Thomas' Parish. Notation: by Banns. p 8

5 October 1802. Washing BALLARD and Elizabeth Thornhill. Married by Rev. George Bingham. p 58

7 March 1795. William BALLARD and Mary Snow. Married by Rev. George Bingham. p 36

30 October 1786. Alexander BALMAINE and Lucy Taylor, dau. Erasmus Taylor, who consents. Sur. Francis Taylor. p 18

17 January 1805. Gerard James BANKS and Ann Davis. Married by Rev. George Bingham. (Gerard, son of Adam Banks, 1742-19 August 1816 m. 1767 Gracey James, both of Madison Co. Gerard d. 1818. 15 T 246.) p 65

22 March 1787. Thomas BARBER and Mary Taylor. Sur. James Taylor. p 19

24 September 1773. Ambrose BARBOUR and Catharine Thomas. Found in Deed Book 17. Catharine of St. Thomas' Parish; Ambrose of Bromfield Parish. p 203

15 October 1795. James BARBOUR and Lucy Johnson. Sur. James Taylor, Jr. Married 20 October by Rev. George Eve. p 38

24 September 1804. Philip Pendleton BARBOUR and Frances T. Johnson. Sur. Thomas Barbour. J. W. Barbour consents for Frances; no relationship stated. Married 4 October by Rev. Hamilton Goss. p 64

28 November 1808. Philip C. S. BARBOUR and Peggy Pollock, dau. William Pollock, who consents. Sur. John Moore. Wit. John Pollock. Married 29 November by Rev. Robert Jones. p 73

22 March 1796. Richard BARBOUR and Mary Moore. Sur. Thomas Barbour, Jr. p 39

- -   1771-74. Thomas BARBOUR and Mary Thomas. This marriage found on a flyleaf of a memorandum book in Orange Court House by J. W. Browning. p 17

12 July 1791. James BARKER and Sarah Maze, widow. Sur. William Rumsey. Wit. Francis Taylor. Married by Rev. Nathaniel Sanders. p 28

29 January 1810. Leonard BARKER and Keturah Robinson, dau. Francis Robinson. Sur. Jesse B. Webb. Wit. William Terrell. Married by Rev. Jeremiah Chandler. p 77

24 September 1772. Nathaniel BARKSDALE and Anne Douglas. This license found in old fee books by J. W. Browning. Both of St. Thomas' Parish. p 2

26 February 1810. Alford BATLEY and Mishel Wright. Sur. Thomas A. Dempsey. Mishel over 21. p 77

- -   1771. WILLIAM BARNETT and Elizabeth Carrer or Carrell. This marriage found on a flyleaf of a memorandum book in Orange Court House by J. W. Browning. p 17

9 June 1790. Lawrence BATTAILE and Ann Hay Taliaferro. Sur. James Taylor. p 26

12 January 1793. Bailey BEACH and Nancy Vaughn, dau. James Vaughn, who consents and is surety. p 31

21 December 1803. Henry BEACH and Delila True, dau. Martin True, who consents for her in person. Sur. Joseph Beach. Married 27 December by Rev. William Calhoun. p 62

17 December 1810. John BEADLES, Jr. and Lucinda Haynes, dau. Jasper Haynes, who writes his consent. Sur. Robert M. Beadles. p 79

5 February 1807. Robert M. BEADLES and Sarah Winslow. Sur. Fortunatus Winslow, who makes oath Sarah is over 21; no relationship stated. p 70

30 May 1786. William BEALE, Jr. and Hannah Gordon, of age and writes her own consent. James Gordon, Jr., brother of Hannah, makes affidavit as to her age. Dau. of John and Hannah Gordon. Sur. John Gordon. p 18

24 July 1797. Bennett BEASLEY and Mary Bryan. Edward Bryan consents for Mary; no relationship stated. Sur. Jeremiah Bryan. p 44

8 June 1791. John BEASELEY and Sally Eaves, dau. William Eaves, who consents and is surety. John is son of Gustin Beasley, who consents. Married 9 June by Rev. Nathaniel Sanders. This name was Augustine Beasley. p 28

1 October 1792. Charles BEAZLEY and Elizabeth Wait. Sur. William Philips and John Davis. Married 30 October by Rev. George Eve. p 31

18 December 1802. John BEAZLEY and Lucy Porter, dau. Abner Porter, who consents. Sur. William Newman. Wit. William Porter. Married 23 December by Rev. Jacob Watts. p 58

21 June 1803. Valentine BEAZLEY and Franky Powell, dau. Joice Powell, who consents. Sur. William L. Powell. Wit. Honour Price Powell. Married 30 June by Rev. George Bingham. p 60

25 December 1797. William BEAZLEY and Betsy Powell, dau. Benjamin Powell, who consents. Sur. Charles Beazley. Wit. John Beazley and James Taylor. p 44

26 December 1805. Richard BECKETT and Nancy Thornhill. Married by Rev. George Bingham. p 67

21 December 1791. Abner BECKHAM and Frances Thomas, dau. Elizabeth Thomas, who consents. Sur. Seth Spencer. Wit. William Thomas and James Taylor, Jr. p 29

16 March 1777. John BEEDLE and Elizabeth Cassen. Found in Deed Book 17. Both in St. Thomas' Parish. Notation: by Banns. p 5

24 June 1809. John BEEKMAN and Rebecca Hancock, dau. William Hancock, who is surety. Married 25 June by Rev. Robert Jones. p 75

17 September 1810. Brockman BELL and Rebecca Brockman, dau. John Brockman, who consents. Sur. Jacob B. Brockman, who makes oath Rebecca is over 21. p 78

19 September 1796. Henry BELL and Susanna Adkins. John Adkins, Jr. and Nancy Adkins consent for Susanna; no relationship stated. Sur. Roger Bell. p 41

4 January 1808. Jacob BELL and Martha H. Taliaferro, dau. Ann Taliaferro of Madison County. Hay Taliaferro, guardian of Martha, consents for her. Sur. John Taliaferro. Wit. Lucy M. Taliaferro. Married by Rev. Isham Tatum. p 72

3 July 1787. John BELL and Judith Burnley. Sur. Reuben Burnley. p 19

4 December 1804. John BELL and Fanny Minton, dau. John Minton, who is surety. p 65

13 May 1793. Patrick BELL and Polly Quisenberry. Sur. Roger Bell. p 33

6 April 1810. Robert W. BELL and Anne T. Schenk. Married by Rev. James Goss. p 78

28 December 1795. Thomas BELL and Sally Burnley. Sur. William Shepherd. Wit. James Taylor, Jr. p 38

30 March 1799. Thomas BELL, Jr. and Lucy Reynolds, dau. William and Elizabeth Reynolds, who consent. Sur. Patrick Bell. Wit. Henry Bell and James Taylor. p 48

19 November 1804. Thomas BELL and Selah Milburn, who writes her own consent. Sur. Robert F. Moore. Wit. Thomas Jenkins, who makes oath Selah is over 21. Married by Rev. William Calhoun. p 64

23 February 1786. William BELL and Elizabeth Cave Johnson, widow, dau. Benjamin Cave. William Bell is a widower. Wit. Ben Johnson and Thomas Barbour. p 18

21 December 1795. William BELL and Rhoda Atkins, dau. John and Susannah Atkins, who consent. Sur. Roger Bell. Wit. James Taylor, Jr. Married 24 December by Rev. Nathaniel Sanders. p 38

16 November 1803. William BELL and Fanny Boston, dau. Reubin Boston, who is surety. William, son of John Bell, who makes oath William is over 21. Married by Rev. William Calhoun. p 61

11 February 1807. William S. BERRY and Rachel Row, dau. Thomas Row, who consents and is surety. Wit. Richard W. Chapman. Married by Rev. Nathaniel Sanders, Baptist. p 70

14 September 1785. Thomas BIBB and Sarah Brockman, dau. Samuel Brockman, Jr., who consents. Sur. Joseph Woolfolk. Wit. William Chiles. p 16

22 November 1791. George BICKERS and Nancy Mallory. Sur. Thomas Dear. Wit. James Taylor, Jr. Married 25 November by Rev. Nathaniel Sanders. p 29

19 March 1805. Joel BICKERS and Rosanna Atkins, dau. John Atkins, who consents and is surety. He also makes oath Joel is over 21. Married 20 March by Rev. Robert Jones. p 66

5 November 1788. John BICKERS and Nancy Landrum, who writes her own consent. Sur. James Taylor. p 22

3 June 1794. William BICKERS and Sally Leathers. Sur. Caleb Bickers. Wit. James Taylor. p 35

28 March 1791. Joseph BISHOP and Ann Clark, dau. John and Mary Clark, who consent. Sur. William Clark. Wit. John Clark. Married 31 March by Rev. Nathaniel Sanders. p 28

28 September 1793. Joseph BISHOP and Jane Terrell, spinster. Sur. Edmund Terrell. Married 29 September by Rev. James Garnett. p 33

4 December 1795. Thaddeus BLACKERLY and Jane Marshall, dau. Merryman Marshall, who consents. Sur. Ellis Hambleton. Wit. John Farguson and David Hening. p 38

23 December 1801. Thomas BLACKERLY and Elizabeth Herring, dau. Thomas Harring. Sur. Thaddeus Blackerly. Wit. Genny Floyd and Polly Herring. Married 24 December by Rev. Jacob Watts. p 55

1 September 1810. Leland BLACKWELL and Nancy Burton, dau. William Burton, who consents. Sur. Robert Burton. Wit. Elizabeth Burton. Married 11 October by Rev. Jacob Watts. p 78

27 April 1791. James BLAIR and Helen Shepherd. Sur. Alexander Shepherd. p 28

10 December 1773. John BLAIR and Elizabeth Smith. Found in Deed Book 17. Both of St. Thomas' Parish. p 203

22 October 1807. James BLAKEY and Nancy Branham, dau. Robert Branham, who is surety. Wit. Reynolds Chapman. Married 11 November by Rev. George Bingham. p 72

30 October 1780. John BLAKEY and Sarah Cowherd, dau. Jonathan Cowherd, who consents. Sur. James Cowherd. Wit. Churchill Blakey. Both of St. Thomas' Parish. p 9

12 February 1807. Reubin BLAKEY and Polly Strother. Married by Rev. William Douglass, Methodist. p 70

18 January 1798. William BLAKEY and Elizabeth Davis, widow, who writes her own consent. Sur. Elijah Graves. Wit. James Taylor. p 45

26 October 1803. Yelverton C. BLAKEY and Judith Burton, dau. Capt. May Burton, who consents. Sur. Alexander Bradford. Wit. Benjamin Burton. The "C" probably stands for Conway. p 61

9 March 1792. John BLANTON and Mary Grady, who writes her own consent. Sur. William Grady, Jr. Married 29 March by Rev. Nathaniel Sanders. p 29

5 June 1797. John BLEDSOE and Polly Dear, dau. Thomas Dear, who consents. Sur. Thomas Williamson. Wit. Derenzy McDaniel, Moses Bledsoe and Bledsoe Brockman. John, son of Aaron Bledsoe, who consents. p 43

14 December 1809. John BLEDSOE and Susanna Pitcher, dau. William Pitcher, Sr., who consents. Sur. Edmund Pitcher. Wit. William Pitcher, Jr. p 76

10 December 1777. Moses BLEDSOE and Ann Perry. Found in Deed Book 17. Both of St. Thomas' Parish. Notation: by Banns. p 6

21 July 1785. William BLEDSOE and Sally Morton, dau. Elijah Morton, who consents. Sur. Aaron Bledsoe. Wit. William Terrell. p 15

12 September 1773. George BLOWS and Catharina Feen (?). Found in Deed Book 17. Catharina of St. Thomas' Parish; George of Augusta County. p 203

26 March 1799. Thomas BOHANNON and Levina Marquess, dau. John Marquess, who consents. Sur. Isaac Pettit. Married 31 March by Rev. Nathaniel Sanders. p 48

19 April 1791. John BOLING, Jr. and Susannah Bell. Thomas Bell consents for Susannah; no relationship stated. Sur. William Boling. p 28

1 October 1788. William BOLING and Phebe Hawkins. Phebe Hawkins Poindexter consents for Phebe; no relationship stated. Sur. James Gaines. Wit. John Boling and Samuel Boling. p 22

5 March 1792. Joseph BOOTH and Polly Grace, dau. George Grace, who consents. Sur. Mark Lampton. p 29

18 December 1809. Reubin BOOTON and Mary Anderson, dau. Jacob Anderson, who is surety. Married 21 December by Rev. George Bingham. See Reuben Boston. p 77

11 May 1796. George BOSTON and Elizabeth Vaughn. Sur. Joseph Vaughn. p 40

19 March 1793. John BOSTON and Frankey Petty, dau. George Petty, who consents. Sur. George Waugh. Wit. Pierce Sanford. p 32

13 January 1803. John BOSTON and Sarah Moseley. Married by Rev. Robert Jones. p 59

13 September 1783. Reuben BOSTON and Sarah Hawkins. Sur. George Petty. Wit. Francis Taylor. p 13

18 December 1809. Reuben BOSTON and Mary Anderson, dau. Jacob Anderson, who is surety. Married 21 December by Rev. George Bingham. See Reubin Booton. p 77

30 January 1778. Robert BOSTON and Lucy Wright. Found in Deed Book 17. Both of St. Thomas' Parish. p 7

31 March 1795. Charles BOSWELL and Lucy Thompson. Sur. Henry Wood. Wit. James Taylor. p 37

1 April 1802. John BOTT and Susanna C. Spotswood. Sur. Robert Spotswood, who makes oath Susanna is over 21. p 57

22 February 1796. Ambrose BOURNE and Jane Newman, dau. Frances Newman, who consents. Sur. William Morton. Wit. George Newman. Married 5 March by Rev. Nathaniel Sanders. p 39

2 January 1757. Francis BOURNE and Frances Christopher. This license found in an old fee book by J. W. Browning. Both of St. Thomas' Parish. p 1

25 November 1799. Tandy BOWCOCK and Judith Douglass, dau. John Douglass, who consents. Wit. John Williams. Married 26 November by Rev. Bartlett Bennett. p 49

16 September 1789. Thomas BOWER and Margaret Landrum. Sur. John Bickers. Wit. James Taylor. p 24

10 October 1791. Charles BOWLING and Sarah McKenney, dau. William McKenney, who consents. Sur. William Thomas. Married 13 October by Rev. Nathaniel Sanders. p 28

22 August 1773. John BOWLING and Mary Ballard. Found in Deed Book 17. Both of St. Thomas' Parish. p 203

16 January 1797. George BOXLEY and Drusilla Graves, dau. Isaac Graves, who consents. Sur. Jonathan Graves. Wit. Claiborne Graves and James Taylor, Jr. p 42

6 March 1801. Thomas BOYER and Martha Thompson, who writes her own consent. Sur. James Williams. Wit. Capt. May Burton, Jr. and Benjamin Williams. Married 8 March by Rev. Hamilton Goss. p 53

18 March 1808. Joseph BRADEN and Polly Neale, dau. Fielding Neale, deceased. James Beazley, uncle and guardian of Polly, consents for her. Sur. James Archer. Wit. James Beazley. Married 22 March by Rev. George Bingham. p 68

16 November 1802. Alexander BRADFORD and Hannah Burton, dau. Capt. May Burton, who consents. Sur. Benjamin Burton, who makes oath Alexander is over 21. Wit. Baldwin M. Buckner. Married 18 November by Rev. William Carpenter, Jr., Lutheran. p 58

29 July 1775. George BRADLEY and Lucy Rice. Found in Deed Book 17. Both of St. Thomas' Parish. Notation: by Banns. p 4

20 October 1803. James BRADLEY and Elizabeth Wells. George Wells consents for Elizabeth; no relationship stated. Sur. John Sleet. Wit. William Wells. Married by Rev. Nathaniel Sanders, Baptist. p 61

16 May 1801. John BRADLEY and Sally Hancock. Sur. William Hancock. Wit. Reynolds Chapman. Married 18 May by Rev. Robert Jones. p 53

15 January 1802. William BRADLEY and Polly Marshall. Sur. Thomas Marshall. Married 18 January by Rev. Hamilton Goss. p 56

1 September 1785. Benjamin BRAGG and Polly Twentyman. Sur. William Jameson. Married 4 September by Rev. John Price. p 16

25 October 1801. Moore BRAGG and Jenny York. Sur. Armistead York. Married 5 November by Rev. Nathaniel Sanders, Baptist. p 55

16 August 1791. Marmaduke BRAMHAM and Fanny Hughes, dau. Francis Hughes, who consents. Sur. Thomas Chisham. Married 18 August by Rev. Nathaniel Sanders. (This name must be Branham.) p 28

5 September 1792. Tavner BRANHAM and Polly Sisson, dau. Sarah Sisson, who consents. Sur. Morgan Finnell. Wit. James Taylor, Jr. p 30

24 August 1786. Patrick BRAY and Mary Stocks, dau. Thomas Stocks, who consents. Sur. Francis Dade. Wit. Margaret McCalaster. p 18

7 December 1789. Ephraim BREEDING and Molly Franklin, dau. Edward Franklin, who consents. Sur. Jonathan Franklin. Wit. James Taylor. p 25

31 July 1790. Richard BREEDING and Elizabeth Franklyn, dau. Edward Franklyn, who consents. Sur. Jonathan Franklyn. Wit. Ephraim Breeding. Double Wedding! See Jonathan Franklyn. p 26

3 January 1809. Broadus BREEDLOVE and Nancy Dovell. Sur. Martin Thomas, who makes oath Nancy is over 21. Married 12 January by Rev. Ambrose Brockman of Albemarle County. p 74

11 February 1784. Madison BREEDLOVE and Judy Buckner. Sur. Francis Bush. Wit. William Moore. In St. Thomas' Parish. p 13

27 November 1809. Nathaniel BREEDLOVE and Elender Mitchell. Sur. William Mitchell. Married by Rev. Ambrose Brockman of Albemarle County. p 76

10 August 1796. William BREEDWELL and Anky Blackwell, widow. Sur. Josua Kendell. Wit. Burrell Levell. William, son of Thomas Breedwell, who consents. p 40

30 October 1808. Kendal C. BRENT and Polly W. Burton, dau. James Burton, who consents. Sur. William Burton, Jr. Wit. Mildred Goodrich, Fanny Burton and William Burton. Married by Rev. Jacob Watts. p 73

30 December 1795. Matthew BRIDGES and Mary Row. Sur. Edmund Row. Married by Rev. Nathaniel Sanders. p 38

4 July 1788. William BRIDGES and Ann Row, dau. Edmund Row, who consents. Sur. Thomas Row. p 22

24 February 1800. Absalom BRIGHTWELL and Winefred Pines. Sur. John Montague. Wit. Charles Bell. Married by Rev. Nathaniel Sanders. p 50

22 April 1793. Andrew BROCKMAN and Amelia Brockman, dau. William Brockman, who consents. Sur. Samuel Brockman. p 32

2 June 1802. Bledsoe BROCKMAN and Elizabeth Landrum, dau. Thomas Landrum, who consents and is surety. p 57

9 January 1795. Elijah BROCKMAN and Sally Tomlinson. Sur. William Tomlinson. p 36

6 December 1790. James BROCKMAN and Nancy Bledsoe. Sur. Aaron Bledsoe. p 27

18 July 1806. James BROCKMAN and Milly Turner. Married by Rev. Robert Jones. p 68

2 December 1788. John BROCKMAN and Nancy Long. Married by Rev. George Eve. This name may be Lang. p 23

9 November 1779. Major BROCKMAN and Mary Patterson, dau. Turner and Susanna Patterson, who consent. Sur. Sam Brockman. Both of St. Thomas' Parish. p 9

25 April 1796. Moses BROCKMAN and Nelly Brockman. Sur. William Dollins. p 40

24 October 1791. Samuel BROCKMAN, Jr. and Nancy Durrett. Sur. Joel Durrett. p 29

23 November 1784. William BROCKMAN and Mary Smith. Sur. George Smith. In St. Thomas' Parish. p 14

23 November 1805. Charles BRONAUGH and Mary Daniel. Sur. Caleb Lindsay, who makes oath Mary is over 21. p 65

3 April 1810. Charles B. BRONAUGH and Elizabeth Brockman, dau. William Brockman, who consents. Sur. Joshua L. Brockman. Wit. James Daniel. p 78

13 March 1789. George BROOK and Dorothy Taylor. Married by Rev. George Eve. p 24

8 April 1788. Robert BROOKING and Patsey Russell, signs her own consent.
Sur. John Scott. Wit. Johnny Scott. Married 11 April by Rev. James
Waddell, Presbyterian. p 21

22 December 1785. Samuel BROOKING and Mary Taylor. Sur. Chapman
Taylor. Wit. James Coleman. p 16

21 January 1778. William BROOKING and Anne Thompson. Found in Deed
Book 17. Both of St. Thomas' Parish. p 7

28 October 1786. Thomas BROUGHTON and Sarah Kamp, writes her own
consent. Sur. James Newman, Jr. Wit. Edmund Henshaw. p 18

11 November 1788. James BROWN and Nancy Harrod. Sur. John Harrod. p 23

10 September 1807. Loudoun B. BRUCE and Milly Estes. Sur. William
Estes, who makes oath Milly is over 21; no relationship stated.
Married by Rev. George Bingham. p 71

21 September 1777. Mordecai BRUCE and Christina Aheart. Found in
Deed Book 17. Both of St. Thomas' Parish. Notation: by Banns. p 5

3 August 1801. Peter BRUNER and Catey Kiblinger. Sur. Daniel Kiblinger.
p 54

15 March 1793. Edward BRYAN and Polly Hambleton. Edward Hambleton
consents for Polly; no relationship stated. Wit. George Gaines and
John Bryan. Sur. William Stowers. Wit. James Taylor. p 32

23 December 1775. Thomas BRYANT and Frankie Thornton. Found in Deed
Book 17. Both of St. Thomas' Parish. Notation: by Banns. p 5

15 December 1796. Anthony BUCK and Mary Shepherd. Sur. Andrew Shepherd,
Jr. Wit. James Taylor, Jr. p 41

27 January 1785. John BUCKHANNAN and Mary Smith. Sur. Henry Smith.
In St. Thomas' Parish. p 14

12 November 1794. Baldwin BUCKNER and Fanny Burton. Sur. James Collins.
Married 16 November by Rev. George Eve. p 36

4 February 1809. Isaac BURKE and Jane Miller. Sur. Robert Miller who
makes oath Jane is over 21; no relationship stated. Married by Rev.
George Bingham. p 75

8 November 1779. Garland BURNLEY and Frances Taylor. Both of St.
Thomas' Parish. Sur. Robert Taylor. p 8

1 November 1798. James BURNLEY and Nancy Parsons, who writes her own
consent. Sur. Andrew Shepherd, Jr. Wit. William C. Webb. p 47

26 July 1772. Richard BURNLEY and Eliza Swan Jones. This license found in old fee book by J. W. Browning. Both of St. Thomas' Parish. p 2

8 January 1790. Roger BURRUS and Cynthia Mills, dau. Nathaniel Mills, who consents. Sur. Roger Tandy. Wit. Henry Tandy. (Cynthia b. 19 September 1772, dau. of Nathaniel and Frances Thompson Mills. Roger son of Thomas 1722-1788 and Frances Tandy Burrus. 15 T 40.) p 25

24 October 1788. Samuel BURRUS and Catey Rucker. Married by Rev. George Eve. p 22

19 January 1779. James BURTON and Mary White. Both of St. Thomas' Parish. Sur. Francis Taylor. Wit. John White and Richard White. Mary, dau. of Jeremiah White, who consents. p 8

2 April 1799. James BURTON and Betsy Goodridge, spinster. Sur. James Taylor. Wit. George Sharman. Married by Rev. Hamilton Goss. Betsy writes her own consent. p 48

27 July 1807. John BURTON and Milly May. Sur. Joel May, who makes oath both are over 21. Married by Rev. Nathaniel Sanders. p 71

29 September 1776. Capt. May BURTON and Sarah Head. Found in Deed Book 17. Both of St. Thomas' Parish. p 7

24 December 1806. William BURTON and Ann Goodrich, who writes her own consent. Sur. William Rucker. Wit. Betsy Burton and Polly W. Burton. Betsy Burton certifies Ann was 21 on 14 December 1806. Married 25 December by Rev. Jacob Watts. p 69

5 September 1798. Edmond BUSH and Elizabeth Warker. Married by Rev. George Bingham. p 46

27 July 1773. Francis BUSH and Lucy Davis. Found in Deed Book 17. Both of St. Thomas' Parish. p 203

22 March 1802. Thomas BUSH and Liddy Breadwell. Sur. Henry Wood. Married 25 March by Rev. Nathaniel Sanders, Baptist. p 57

16 September 1803. James CAMP and Mary Wood. Married by Rev. Robert Jones. p 61

27 November 1772. William CAMP and Frances Willis. Found in Deed Book 17. 1 December indicates that was the day of the marriage. William Camp of Culpeper County. p 2

1 November 1786. Archibald CAMPBELL and Susannah Arnold. Sur. William Hancock. p 18

25 September 1773. Abraham CARD and Ann Archer. Found in Deed Book 17. Both of St. Thomas' Parish. p 203

14 January 1783. Jacob CARROL and Tabitha Reynolds. Sur. Benjamin Griffy. Wit. Joseph Reynolds and John Faulconer. Rachel Reynolds consents for Tabitha; no relationship stated. p 12

23 April 1792. Joseph CARTER and Polly Bell. Sur. John Carter. p 30

24 March 1788. William CASEY and Agnes Taylor. Charles Taylor consents for Agnes; no relationship stated. Sur. Jeremiah Sims. Married 6 April by Rev. George Eve. p 21

17 February 1795. William CASON and Mary Thompson, dau. John and Catherine Thompson, who consent. Sur. Frederick Thompson. Wit. Henry Allen, Joel Underwood and Walker Raines. p 36

8 January 1803. Abner CAVE and Betsey Sims, dau. William Sims, who consents. Sur. Thomas Cave. Wit. James Sims and Sanders Walker. Married by Rev. George Bingham. Abner, son of William Cave, Sr. p 59

22 December 1796. Bartlett CAVE, Jr. and Jenny Snow. Married by Rev. George Bingham. p 41

21 January 1794. Benjamin CAVE, Jr. and Elizabeth White. Sur. Willliam White. Wit. James Taylor, Jr. Married 22 January by Rev. George Eve. p 34

25 November 1805. Richard CAVE and Maria Porter. Sur. Abner Porter. Married by Rev. Robert Jones. p 67

12 December 1806. Richard CAVE and Lucy Shelton. Married by Rev. Nathaniel Sanders, Baptist. p 69

19 August 1806. Robert CAVE and Lucy Bradley. Sur. George Bradley, Jr., who makes oath both are over 21; no relationship stated. Married by Rev. Robert Jones. p 69

4 November 1797. Thomas CAVE and Nancy Sims. Sur. William Sims. Wit. James Taylor. p 44

28 December 1761. William CAVE and Mary Mallory. This license found in an old fee book by J. W. Browning. Both of St. Thomas' Parish. p 1

6 June 1783. William CAVE and Frances Christy, dau. Julius Christy, who consents. Sur. Belfield Cave. Wit. William Glass, John Gulley and P. Kavenaugh. Married 11 June by Rev. George Eve. William Cave of Brumfield Parish, Culpeper County, son of John Cave. Frances of St. Thomas' Parish. p 12

22 November 1791. William CAVE and Judy Jollett. Sur. James Jollett. Mary Jollett consents for Judy; no relationship stated. p 29

13 July 1810. William CAVE and Sarah Snow. Sur. Bartlett Cave, who makes oath Sarah is over 21. Married 16 July by Rev. George Bingham. p 78

17 November 1790. Abraham CHAMBERS and Mary Dawson, dau. John Dawson, who consents. Sur. William Dawson. Wit. John Chissam and Gabriel Chissam. Married 18 November by Rev. Nathaniel Sanders. p 27

15 July 1790. Thomas CHAMBERS and Milly Robinson, dau. Artemus Robinson, who consents. Sur. Francis Hughes. Wit. Francis Taylor. p 26

22 December 1789. James CHANDLER and Frances McNeal, dau. Martha McNeal, who consents. Sur. Samuel Thompson, Jr. Wit. James Taylor. p 25

26 December 1791. John CHANDLER and Elizabeth Terrell. Sur. William Lindsay. Wit. Joseph Chandler and James Chandler. William Terrell consents for Elizabeth; no relationship stated. p 29

15 January 1794. Joseph CHANDLER and Nancy Homs, who writes her own consent. Sur. George Scott. Wit. George Coot and Sarah Coot. p 34

24 February 1774. Robert CHANDLER and Suckey Robinson. Found in Deed Book 17. Notation: by Banns. Both of St. Thomas' Parish. p 2

23 November 1803. Thomas CHAPMAN and Elizabeth Early, dau. James Early. Sur. Henry White. Wit. John Early. Married 29 November by Rev. George Bingham. p 61

28 January 1779. James CHILES and Jenny Land. Both of St. Thomas' Parish. Sur. John Leathers. p 8

1 December 1789. James CHISHAM and Catherine Ranes. Sur. Francis Hughes. Wit. James Taylor. p 24

27 August 1796. Benjamin CHISIM and Elizabeth Beckham, dau. Henry Backman, who consents. Sur. John York. Wit. William Wright. p 41

11 December 1788. Lorimer CHOWNING and Judith Carter, who writes her own consent. Sur. George Sharman. Wit. Charles Parrott and George Berry. p 23

1 November 1797. Ambrose CLARK and Mary Thomas, dau. Joseph Thomas, who consents and is surety. Wit. James Taylor, Jr. p 44

25 March 1805. Henry CLARK and Elizabeth Johnson (widow), who writes her own consent. Sur. Thomas Grasty. Wit. William Bickers. p 66

5 March 1804. James CLARK and Sally Payne. Sur. Gabriel Payne, who makes oath Sally is over 21; no relationship stated. Married 20 March by Rev. Nathaniel Sanders, Baptist. p 62

5 February 1807. James CLARK and Elizabeth Graves. Married by Rev. William Douglass, Methodist. p 70

5 November 1794. John CLARK and Winney Powell, dau. John Powell, who consents. Sur. Adam Manspoile. Winney writes her own consent, also. p 35

27 August 1804. John CLARK and Dillah Payne. John Clark, guardian of Dillah, consents for her. Sur. Ikey Richards. p 64

30 January 1797. Larkin CLARK and Rebecca Bell, dau. Thomas and Sally Bell, who consent. Sur. Roger Bell. Wit. John Bowling and James Taylor, Jr. p 42

8 February 1804. Nathaniel CLARK and Nancy Hall. Married by Rev. George Bingham. p 62

16 December 1801. Reubin CLARK and Martha E. Clark, dau. Joseph Clark. Sur. Larkin Clark. Wit. Larkin and Mary Clark. Married 17 December by Rev. Isham Tatum. p 55

31 January 1801. Reuben CLARK and Lizey Petty, dau. George Petty, who consents. Sur. Abner Petty. p 53

28 December 1801. Henry CLARKE and Nanney Grasty. Sur. G. L. Grasty. Married 5 January 1802 by Rev. Nathaniel Sanders, Baptist. p 55

26 January 1802. Walker CLARKE and Elizabeth Vawter, dau. William Vawter, who consents. Sur. Thomas Landrum. Wit. John Lanses. p 56

7 November 1792. William CLARKE and Betsey Cook, spinster. Sur. Edward Pagett. p 31

29 June 1789. Arselm CLARKSON and Milly Jones. Sur. Thomas James. p 24

17 May 1794. Philip CLAYTON and Elizabeth Hackley Stubblefield, dau. George Stubblefield, who consents. Sur. Daniel F. Strother. Wit. James Taylor. p 35

15 February 1791. Jeremiah COATS and Sally Webster, widow. Sur. Francis Weatherall. Wit. James Taylor. p 27

27 March 1783. John COATES and Sarah Thompson. Both of St. Thomas' Parish. Sur. Edward Thompson. p 12

23 January 1776. Robert COCKBURN and Sarah Brown. Found in Deed Book 17. Both of St. Thomas' Parish. Notation: by Banns. p 6

9 April 1774. Patrick COCKRANE and Wintifred Spencer. Found in Deed Book 17. Notation: by Banns. Both of St. Thomas' Parish. p 2

29 January 1785. Ralph COGWELL and Sarah Reynolds, who writes her own consent. Sur. John Dawson. Wit. Tabitha Carrol. Married 1 February by Rev. Nathaniel Sanders. p 14

24 April 1810. Ambrose COLEMAN and Fanny Hilman, dau. Joseph Hilman, who is surety. p 78

7 January 1786. Francis COLEMAN and Betty Davis, dau. Joseph and Elizabeth Davis, who consents. Sur. Francis Taylor. Wit. John Bell and George Davis. p 18

14 April 1780. James COLEMAN and Sarah Taylor, spinster. Both of St. Thomas' Parish. Sur. Moses Hayes. p 9

18 December 1786. James COLEMAN and Milly Chew. Sur. James Taylor. p 19

19 December 1794. John COLEMAN and Elizabeth Bradley. Sur. Samuel Smith. George and Lucy Bradley consent for Elizabeth; no relationship stated. Married 24 December by Rev. George Eve. p 36

24 November 1800. Robert COLEMAN and Sarah Coleman, dau. Elizabeth Coleman, who consents. Sur. Thomas Coleman. Wit. Alexander Penn and Reynolds Chapman. p 52

28 June 1781. Thomas COLEMAN and Susannah Hawkins, widow. Both of St. Thomas' Parish. Sur. James Taylor. p 10

24 May 1781. Edward COLLINS and Anne Collins. Sur. James Coleman. Both of St. Thomas' Parish. p 10

26 April 1794. Francis COLLINS and Peggy Dohoney. Sur. Gideon Underwood. Thomas Dohoney consents for Peggy; no relationship stated. Married 27 April by Rev. George Eve. p 35

10 February 1794. George COLLINS and Elizabeth Mitchell. Sur. William Mitchell. Wit. James Taylor and Charles Taylor. p 34

13 January 1792. James COLLINS and Sarah Harvie, of age, dau. John Harvie, who consents. Sur. William Mitchell. Wit. William Harvie. George Collins, father of James, consents for him. p 29

26 August 1793. James COLLINS and Lucy Burton, dau. Capt. May Burton, Jr., who consents. Sur. William Rucker, Jr. Wit. Joseph Burton and William Rucker. p 33

4 January 1803. John COLLINS and Elizabeth Kirtley. Married by Rev. George Bingham. p 59

28 December 1803. John COLLINS and Betty Yager, who writes her own consent. Sur. Benjamin Collins. p 62

24 December 1792. Lewis Dillard COLLINS and Elizabeth Williams. Sur. Jacob Williams. p 31

13 May 1807. Reubin COLLINS and Fanny Riddle, dau. James Riddle, who consents. Sur. Valentine Riddle. Wit. William Riddle. Married 21 May by Rev. George Bingham. p 70

7 February 1809. Tandy COLLINS and Ann Beazley, dau. James Beazley, Sr., who consents. Sur. Sanford Beazley. Wit. Robert Beazley. Married 9 February by Rev. Jacob Watts. p 75

16 September 1776. William COLLINS and Patty Snell. Found in Deed Book 17. Both of St. Thomas' Parish. Notation: by Banns. p 7

8 November 1804. Preston COLYER and Eliza Hayna. Married by Rev. George Bingham. p 64

20 November 1776. John CONNER and Lucy Daniel. Found in Deed Book 17. Both of St. Thomas' Parish. Sur. James Taylor, Jr. Lucy, dau. of Reuben Daniel, who consents. p 7

7 February 1785. John CONNOR and Mary Lancaster, dau. Mary Lancaster, who consents. Sur. Robert Lancaster, Jr. Wit. Uriah Proctor and John Lancaster. In St. Thomas' Parish. p 15

26 September 1810. Catlett CONWAY, Jr. and Verlinda Taliaferro. Sur. George Conway. (Catlett Conway born 1786, died 25 July 1839, son of Capt. Catlett and Susanna (Fitzhugh) Conway of "Hawfield".) p 78

10 April 1797. Thomas COOK and Mary Chiles, who signs her own consent. Sur. Reuben Garton. Wit. Charles Bell. p 43

13 June 1785. William COOK and Susannah Garton, dau. Uriah Garton, who consents. Sur. William Page. p 15

16 May 1796. Elijah COOKE and Polly Turner, dau. Ann Turner, who consents. Sur. Samuel Hill. Wit. Francis Turnley and John Turner. p 40

18 December 1804. Benjamin COOPER and Susannah Lancaster, dau. John Lancaster, who consents. Sur. William Robinson. Wit. Peter Mason. p 65

18 December 1798. James COOPER and Mildred Smith, dau. James Smith, who consents. Sur. Elisha Adams. Wit. Charles Bell.

24 November 1787. William COOPER and Mary Quisenberry, dau. Moses Quisenberry, who consents. Sur. James Quisenberry. Wit. George Quisenberry. p 20

24 October 1803. Charles COPPEDGE and Lydia Wayt, dau. James Wayt, who consents and is surety. Wit. James Wayt, Jr. Married by Rev. Jacob Watts. p 61

10 March 1790. Augustin CORNELIUS and Sarah Terrell, dau. Peggy Terrell, who consents. Sur. Edmund Terrell. Wit. Charles Cornelius and Joseph Clark. p 26

25 January 1808. Peter COTTOM and Judith Robinson Grynes. John R. Grymes makes oath Judith is over 21; no relationship stated. Sur. James Pulliam. p 72

1 August 1785. Daniel COWGILL and Betsy Martin, dau. Ann Bowen. Sur. John Bowen (step-father?). p 15

15 September 1792. George COWGILL and Phebe Wait, who writes her own consent. Sur. Edward Wait. Wit. James Taylor. p 31

3 May 1794. Isaac COWGILL and Sally Gillock, dau. Elizabeth Gillock, who consents. Sur. Lawrence Gillock. Wit. James Taylor. Married 15 May by Rev. James Garnett. p 35

13 August 1787. Francis COWHERD and Lucy Scott, dau. Johnny Scott, who consents and is surety. p 20

28 June 1794. Reuben COWHERD and Frances Woolfolk, dau. Thomas Woolfolk, who consents. Sur. James Taylor, Sr. Wit. Y. Cowherd. p 35

3 January 1803. Joab COX and Lucy Estes. Sur. William Estes, who makes oath Lucy is over 21; no relationship stated. p 59

6 February 1782. John COX and Mary Bryson, spinster. Both of St. Thomas' Parish. Sur. John Bell. p 11

10 March 1783. Thomas COX and Milley Olliver, dau. Tabitha Olliver, who consents. Sur. Joel Stodghill. Wit. Richard White. Both of St. Thomas' Parish. p 12

29 January 1791. William COX and Betsey Estes, spinster. Sur. John Bell. p 27

25 April 1796. James CRASK and Jane Collins. Sur. Edward Collins. p 39

28 May 1792. Jeremiah CRAWFORD and Jany Crawford, dau. Archelan Crawford, who consents. Sur. Claiborne Rucker. Married 31 May by Rev. George Eve. p 30

9 December 1801. Martin CRAWFORD and Susanna Lamb. Married by Rev. George Bingham. p 55

2 February 1790. Jacob CREW and Martha Dollins, "21 years of age", writes her own consent. Sur. William Dollins. Wit. James Taylor. p 25

17 August 1792. Aaron CROSTHWAIT and Nelly Brockman, dau. John Brockman, who consents. Sur. Caleb Lindsay. Wit. Roger Burrus. p 30

8 November 1802. Joseph CROXTON and Delphy Turner. Sur. Ezekiel Turner, who makes oath both are over 21. p 58

12 April 1757. Benjamin CRUMP and Mary Barber Price. This license found in old fee book by J. W. Browning. After the date 1757 appears in parenthesis (1756). Also Barber corrected to Barbour. Both of St. Thomas' Parish. p 1

8 January 1799. Thomas CRUTCHFIELD and Ann Pendleton Taylor. Sur. James Taylor. p 48

23 January 1801. Elijah CURTIS and Nancy Daniel. Sur. John D. Long. Wit. Reynolds Chapman. p 53

13 March 1782. Francis DADE and Sarah Taliaferro, dau. Lawrence Taliaferro, who consents. Sur. Hay Taliaferro. Wit. Townshend Dade. Both of St. Thomas' Parish. p 11

6 November 1792. William DADE and Sarah Dade, who writes her own consent. Sur. Townshend Dade. William Dade of Prince William County. p 31

23 June 1800. John DALTON and Polly Earles. Sur. Rodham Earles. Married 24 June by Rev. Hamilton Goss. p 51

28 February 1786. Beverly DANIEL and Jane Hiatt. Sur. Benjamin Hiatt. p 18

6 April 1793. Cornelius O. DANIEL and Peggy Plunkett, widow. Sur. John O. Bryan. p 32

5 April 1772. James DANIEL and Lucy Davis. This license found in old fee book by J. W. Browning. p 2

8 April 1797. James DANIEL and Alise Finnell. Sur. James Daniel (?). p 43

25 July 1776. John DANIEL and Lucy Mary Marshall. Sur. Thomas Bell. Found in Deed Book 17. p 6

7 November 1760. Reuben DANIEL and Elizabeth Merry. This license found in an old fee book by J. W. Browning. Both of St. Thomas' Parish. (I think she was widow of Thoms Merry nee Stevens.) p 1

21 December 1804. Reuben R. DANIEL and Elizabeth Reynolds. Sur. Thomas Daniel, who makes oath both are over 21; no relationship stated. (Elizabeth, dau. William and Nancy (Nixon) Reynolds and granddau. of Joseph and Elizabeth (Herndon) Reynolds.) p 65

23 November 1772. Robert DANIEL and Frances Head Humphries. Found in old fee book by J. W. Browning. Page 203 says "Found in Deed Book 17." p 2

31 January 1785. William DANIEL and Mary Gaines, who writes her own consent. Sur. Henry Childs. Wit. James Daniel. (William Daniel b. 12 May 1761; served the Revolution, commissioned Lieutenant July 1787. 14 T 161.) p 14

15 November 1796. Adam DARBY and Catherine Shepherd, dau. Andrew Shepherd, who consents. Sur. Daniel Grinnon, Jr. p 41

19 December 1797. Abraham DARNELL and Elizabeth Darnell. Abraham Darnell, Sr. consents for both. Sur. George McDaniel. Wit. John Payne, John Robertson and Thomas Darnell. Married 20 December by Rev. Hamilton Goss. p 44

23 January 1809. Nelson DARNELL and Cintha Mallory, dau. Henry Mallory, who is surety and makes oath Cintha is over 21. Married 24 January by Rev. Robert Jones. p 75

25 December 1804. Rice DARNELL and Polly Ahart. Married by Rev. Hamilton Goss. p 65

13 August 1794. Thomas DARNELL and Elizabeth Ehart, dau. Catain (?) Gaines (?). Sur. James Alexander. Wit. James Ehart. Married 21 August by Rev. George Martin. p 35

25 August 1776. Alexander DAUNEY and Sally Bell. Found in Deed Book 17. Both of St. Thomas' Parish. p 7

25 December 1796. Absalem DAVIS and Jerusha Davis. Married by Rev. George Bingham. p 41

31 January 1799. Bartlett DAVIS and Sally Lowry. Married by Rev. George Bingham. p 48

25 January 1806. Benjamin DAVIS and Jane Jones. Married by Rev. William Douglass, Methodist. p 68

24 December 1806. Elijah DAVIS and Elizabeth Jones. Married by Rev.
George Bingham. p 69

1 March 1780. James DAVIS and Mary Johnson, who writes her own consent.
Sur. John Bell. Wit. Jonathan Davis and William Bell. p 9

25 August 1785. James DAVIS and Ann Modiset, dau. Mary Modiset, widow.
Sur. Patrick Cochran. Wit. James Taylor. Original bond says
17 August. p 15

21 December 1794. Jickenias DAVIS and Babby Lowry. Married by Rev.
George Bingham. p 36

25 February 1772. John DAVIS and Mary Jones. This license found in old
fee book by J. W. Browning. Both of St. Thomas' Parish. p 2

27 July 1789. John DAVIS and Mary Eastin. Sur. Reuben Eastin. p 24

1 January 1776. Leonard DAVIS and Susanna Burrows. Found in Deed
Book 17. Both of St. Thomas' Parish. Notation: by Banns. p 6

24 April 1783. Thomas DAVIS and Elizabeth Early, dau. Theodosia Early,
who consents. Sur. James Early. Wit. William Davis and Thomas
White. Both of St. Thomas' Parish. p 12

10 January 1789. Thomas DAVIS and Elizabeth Pannill, dau. William
Pannill, Sr., who consents. Sur. William Pannill, Jr. p 23

5 February 1789. William DAVIS and Nancy Easton. Married by Rev.
George Eve. p 23

27 November 1809. William DAVIS and Sally Boston, dau. Reuben Boston,
who is surety. p 76

3 December 1803. James DAWSON and Nancy Hughes, dau. Francis Hughes.
Alexander Hughes makes oath both are over 21. Sur. Marmaduke
Branham. Wit. Reynolds Chapman, Clerk. Married by Rev. Nathaniel
Sanders, Baptist. p 61

19 October 1775. John DAWSON and Anne Chism. Found in Deed Book 17.
Both in St. Thomas' Parish. Notation: by Banns. p 4

3 August 1795. John DAWSON and Nancy Pollard, who writes her own
consent. Sur. Benjamin Hawkins. Married 25 August by Rev. Nathaniel
Sanders. p 37

31 May 1757. Musgrove DAWSON and Mary Waugh. This license found in an
old fee book by J. W. Browning. Groom designated by the word clerk
in parenthesis (Clerk). Both of St. Thomas' Parish. p 1

18 August 1790. John DEANE and Elizabeth Mays. Sur. Zachary Jones.
Married by Rev. Nathaniel Sanders. p 26

2 June 1789. William DEANE and Sarah Boston. Sur. Joseph Boston. Wit.
James Taylor. p 24

1 November 1774. John DEAR and Catherine Smith. Found in Deed Book 17.
Both of St. Thomas' Parish. Notation: by Banns. p 3

27 January 1778. Thomas DEAR and Lucy Fennell. Found in Deed Book 17.·
Both of St. Thomas Parish. Notation: by Banns. p 7

19 June 1783. Thomas DEERING and Mary Rumsey, of lawful age. Sur. James
Deering. Mary Treasey consents for Mary; no relationship stated.
p 12

5 March 1773. John DELANY and Susannah Watts. Found in Deed Book 17.
Susannah of St. Thomas' Parish; John of Bromfield Parish. p 203

7 September 1785. Lavey DEREY and Ann Wye, who writes her own consent.
Sur. James Head. p 16

11 February 1787. Robert DICKENSON and Ruth Parish, dau. Joseph Parish,
who consents. Sur. William Robinson. Wit. J. Williamson and John
Jones. p 19

22 October 1810. Thomas DICKINSON and Nancy Wood, dau. Hopefull Wood,
who consents. Sur. Reubin Twyman. Wit. James Dickenson. p 78

3 October 1773. Samuel DIXON and Charlotte Brown. Found in Deed Book
17. Both of St. Thomas' Parish. p 203

31 December 1792. John DOD and Susanna Lee. Sur. Zachariah Wood. Wit.
James Taylor. This bond is made out in the name of William Dod.
See William Dod. p 31

31 December 1792. William DOD and Susanna Lee. Sur. Zachariah Wood.
Wit. James Taylor. The groom signs the bond as John Dod. See John
Dod. p 31

9 June 1803. James DODD and Nancy Cook. Married by Rev. Nathaniel
Sanders, Baptist. p 60

13 February 1804. John DODD and Sally Johnson. Sur. William Dodd, who
makes oath both are over 21; no relationship stated. p 62

23 February 1775. James DOHONY and Wintifred Vawter. Found in Deed
Book 17. Both of St. Thomas' Parish. Notation: by Banns. p 3

19 October 1790. Rhodes DOHONEY and Jenney Chapman. Joseph Chapman consents for Jenney; no relationship stated. Sur. Francis Collins. p 26

30 December 1789. Reuben DOLLINS and Elizabeth Hensley, dau. William Hensley, who consents. Sur. Lewis Hensley. Wit. John Dollins. p 25

14 March 1803. John DONATHAN and Polly Eluck. Sur. George Smith, who makes oath both are over 21. Married by Rev. Nathaniel Sanders. p 60

27 January 1790. John DONOVER and Sally Gaer, dau. Nathaniel Gaer, who consents. Sur. William Gaer. Wit. Ransdom Gaer. p 25

15 March 1791. Thomas DOOLING and Elizabeth Finnell. Sur. John Gwinn. p 27

13 November 1773. William DOSWELL and Elizabeth Mills. Found in Deed Book 17. Elizabeth of Frederickville Parish; William of Amelia County. p 203

25 April 1796. Charles DOUGLASS and Nancy Payne. Sur. John Payne. Wit. Charles Bell. p 40

28 February 1803. William DUKE and Lini Gibbs. Sur. John H. Gibbs, who makes oath Lini is over 21; no relationship stated. p 59

26 May 1772. Joseph DUNCAN and Nancy Stephens. This license found in old fee book by J. W. Browning. Both of St. Thomas' Parish. p 2

24 January 1775. William DUNN and Mary Bledsoe. Found in Deed Book 17. Both of St. Thomas' Parish. Notation: by Banns. p 3

25 September 1805. Achilles DURRETT and Lydia Quisenberry. Sur. Moses Quisenberry, who makes oath Lydia is over 21; no relationship stated. p 67

20 November 1797. John D. DURRETT and Frances Davis. Sur. James Watts. p 44

6 May 1802. Killam DURRETT and Elizabeth Thomeson. Married by Rev. Robert Jones. p 57

23 June 1772. Joel EARLY and Lucy Smith. This license found in old fee book by J. W. Browning. Both of St. Thomas' Parish. p 2

5 June 1798. Edward EASTHAM and Ann Thornton. George Thornton consents for Ann; no relationship stated. Sur. William Rucker, Jr. Wit. Peter Thornton and Charles Bell. p 46

28 April 1785. John EASTIN and Sarah Griffith, spinster. Sur. David Griffith. p 15

23 March 1782. Philip EASTIN and Elizabeth Henderson, dau. Alexander Henderson, who consents. Sur. William Tomlinson. Wit. Benjamin Johnson and Joseph Smith. Both of St. Thomas' Parish. p 11

2 April 1773. Stephen EASTING and Susannah Johnson. Found in Deed Book 17. Both of St. Thomas' Parish. p 203

26 December 1799. John EASTIS and Sarah Cox, 21 years of age. Sur. Joan Cox. Wit. Charles Bell. p 50

8 January 1798. William EAVES and Nancy Highlander, dau. George High-lander, who consents. Nancy writes her own consent, also. Sur. George Webster. Wit. Betsy Olive. p 45

12 February 1798. Elijah EDDINS and Nancy Osborne, dau. Robert Osborne, who consents. Sur. George Collins. Wit. James Gillum and Sinkler Osborne. Married 15 February by Rev. Hamilton Goss. p 45

31 December 1808. Joseph EDDINS, Jr. and Nancy Davis, dau. Mary Davis, who consents. Sur. Joseph Davis. Wit. Henry Snyder. Married 3 January 1809 by Rev. Jacob Watts. p 74

25 December 1798. Thomas EDDINS and Frances Collins, dau. William Collins, who consents. Sur. John Herndon. Wit. George Collins. Married 26 December by Rev. Hamilton Goss. p 47

24 September 1798. Edmund EDINGTON and Priscilla Gordon. Sur. Samuel Gordon. p 46

28 August 1798. Elisha EDWARDS and Elizabeth Eaton. Sur. William Eaton. Elisha, son of William Edwards, who consents. Wit. Charles Bell. p 46

11 June 1803. Albin ELLIOTT and Urcilla Gaines. Sur. William Roberson, who makes oath Urcella is over 21. p 60

17 January 1785. Richard EMBREE and Judith Payne. Sur. George Payne. In St. Thomas' Parish. p 14

6 August 1810. Abraham ESTES and Sally W. Cox. Sur. William Cox, who makes oath Sally is over 21; no relationship stated. Married 26 August by Rev. George Bingham. p 78

22 July 1776. Samuel ESTES and Wintifred Holladay. Found in Deed Book 17. Both of St. Thomas' Parish. Notation: by Banns. p 6

23 October 1804. William ESTES and Polly Harvey. Sur. Anthony Harvey, who makes oath both are over 21; no relationship stated. p 64

20 March 1809. John EVANS and Nancy King, dau. Julian King, who is surety; also makes oath John is over 21. Married 24 March by Rev. Robert Jones. p 75

19 August 1799. Joseph EVE and Polly Smith, dau. Raif and Patty Smith, who consent. Sur. John Smith. Wit. James Taylor. p 49

18 March 1805. Thomas EVES and Fanny Jenkins, dau. William Jenkins, who consents. Sur. James Atkins. Wit. Thomas Atkins. p 66

29 May 1797. Thomas FALLIS and Polly James. Sur. James Coleman. p 43

1 February 1806. John T. FANT and Fanny James, dau. Joseph and Lucy James, who consent. Sur. Joseph James. Married 18 February by Rev. Nathaniel Sanders, Baptist. p 68

12 May 1788. John FARGUSON and Frances Lucas. William Lucas consents for Frances and is surety; no relationship stated. p 21

15 November 1803. Vivion FARGUSON and Mary A. Mills, dau. Nathaniel Mills. Sur. Jackson Mills. Wit. Charles Mills. (Mary Ann Mills b. 16 November 1780. Vivion, son of William and Margaret (Vivion) Farguson. 15 T 41.) p 61

30 March 1794. David FAULCONER and Sarah Grady, dau. William Grady, who consents. Sur. John Partlow. Wit. George Faulconer and Richard Faulconer. p 35

27 November 1802. Elias FAULCONER and Polly Neuman, who writes her own consent. Sur. Robert B. Long, who makes oath both are over 21. Wit. Nicholas Faulconer. p 58

23 June 1794. James FAULCONER and Milly Sisson. Sayrey (Sarah) Sisson consents for Milly; no relationship stated. Sur. Morgan Finnell. p 35

16 January 1775. John FAULCONER and Margaret Morrison. Found in Deed Book 17. Both of St. Thomas' Parish. Wit. Richard Reynolds and William Strother. Taliaferro Craig, guardian and executor of Margaret, consents for her. p 3

18 December 1804. Nicholas FAULCONER and Frances Faulconer, who writes her own consent. Sur. Reubin Faulconer. Wit. John Faulconer and Spencer Faulconer. p 65

1 November 1796. Reuben FAULCONER and Jenny Faulconer, dau. Thomas Faulconer, who consents. Sur. John Mason. Wit. David Faulconer and George Faulconer. p 41

9 April 1792. Richard FAULCONER and Nancy Sanders, dau. Nathaniel Sanders, who consents. Sur. William Fisher. Wit. James Taylor. p 30

14 May 1798. Samuel FAULCONER and Sarah Burges, who writes her own consent. Sur. Edmund Burges. p 46

23 January 1797. William FAULCONER and Betsy Chisholm. Sur. William Dawson. p 42

8 June 1793. George FAULKNER and Nancy Coleman, dau. James Coleman, who consents. Sur. Thomas Shadrich. Wit. David Faulkner. p 33

19 February 1776. Thomas FEARNEY and Agy Lucas. Found in Deed Book 17. Both of St. Thomas' Parish. Notation: by Banns. p 6

19 November 1775. William FEARNEY and Sarah Morton. Found in Deed Book 17. Both in St. Thomas' Parish. Notation: by Banns. p 4

9 November 1775. Charles FENNEL and Nancy Saunders. Found in Deed Book 17. Both in St. Thomas' Parish. Notation: by Banns. p 4

5 February 1778. William FENNELL, Jr. and Jeany Bourn. Found in Deed Book 17. Both of St. Thomas' Parish. p 7

13 May 1795. George FERRELL and Polly Wolf, dau. Leonard Wolf, who consents. Sur. Joseph Canterberry. Wit. Robert Russell Hill. Leonard signs his name Woolf. p 37

26 September 1794. John FERRELL and Caty Miller. Sur. William Brockman. p 35

1 January 1799. Henry FILLINGER and Betsy Ferrell. Married by Rev. Hamilton Goss. p 48

25 August 1775. Benjamin FINNELL and Sarah Carter Sleet, widow. Found in Deed Book 17. Both of St. Thomas' Parish. p 4

28 December 1799. Benjamin FINNELL and Elizabeth Robinson, dau. Artemus and Pheby Robinson, who consent. Sur. Moses Robinson. Wit. Thomas Chambers and Reynolds Chapman. Consent is signed Artemenus Robinson. p 50

27 January 1794. George FINNELL and Sally Dawson, who writes her own consent. Sur. Lawrence Gillock. Wit. James Taylor. p 34

13 June 1791. James FINNELL and Rebecca Chambers. Sur. Marmaduke Branham. James, son of Simon Finnell, who consents for him. Married by Rev. Nathaniel Sanders. Return dated 18 August. p 33

2 February 1797. John FINNELL and Catey Surry, who writes her own consent. Sur. James Finnell. Wit. Charles Bell and James Taylor. p 42

11 January 1798. John FINNELL and Elizabeth Chambers, spinster. Sur. James Finnell. Wit. James Taylor. p 45

13 December 1784. Reuben FINNELL and Elizabeth Bourne, dau. Henry Bourne, who consents. Sur. John Leathers. Wit. William Leathers. Married by Rev. Nathaniel Sanders. p 14

26 December 1805. James FISHER and Fanny Mason. Sur. Peter Mason, Jr., who makes oath Fanny is over 21; no relationship stated. Married by Rev. Nathaniel Sanders. p 68

28 January 1802. Eason FITZGERAL and Mary Self. Married by Rev. George Bingham. p 56

14 November 1787. Stephen FITZGERRELL and Catherine Bruce. Sur. William Fitzgerrell. Wit. Jacob Ahart. Stephen, son of James Fitzgerrell. p 20

12 March 1804. Battaile FITZHUGH and Elizabeth Taliaferro. Sur. Lawrence Taliaferro. p 62

17 April 1792. Henry FITZHUGH, Jr. and Elizabeth Conway. Sur. Charles Taylor. Wit. Henry Fitzhugh. John B. Fitzhugh, guardian of Henry Fitzhugh, Jr., consents for him. p 30

24 February 1783. William FITZHUGH and Ann Taliaferro, dau. Lawrence Taliaferro, who consents. Sur. Francis Dade. Wit. Hay Taliaferro. Both of St. Thomas' Parish. p 12

14 October 1795. Andrew FLEAK and Frances Rhoads, dau. Epaphroditus Rhoads, who consents. Sur. James Riddle. Married 22 October by Rev. George Eve. p 38

6 May 1797. Henry FLECK and Betsy Smatts. Sur. Peter Sekle. p 43

8 November 1793. Andrew FLEEK and Rachel Lower, who writes her own consent. Sur. John Coleman. Wit. Michael Lower. p 34

5 January 1807. Washington FLETCHER and Elizabeth Payne. Sur. Willis Overton. Married by Rev. Nathaniel Sanders, Baptist. p 70

17 December 1807. William FLETCHER and Delila Sullivan, dau. William Sullivan, who consents. Sur. Gusty Pates. Wit. Lucy Sullivan. Married by Rev. Nathaniel Sanders, Baptist. p 72

4 June 1796. John FLICK and Barbary Kiblinger. Sur. Jacob Kiblinger. Married 9 June by Rev. George Eve. p 40

5 September 1798. William FLICK and Catherine Lower, dau. Michael Lower, Sr., who consents. Sur. Charles Percey. Wit. Jacob and Susannah Schwartzwald. p 46

16 April 1799. Samuel FLOYD and Jane Hering, dau. Thomas Hering, who consents. Sur. Thomas Brady. Wit. William Brady, James Taylor and Hamilton Goss. p 48

FORD: see FOARD

12 December 1785. William FOARD (Ford) and Ann Moore, who writes her own consent. Sur. Reubin Boston. Wit. Finlasson Sleet and James Sleet. Married 14 December by Rev. John Price. p 16

11 January 1792. Absalom FORD and Molly Ransdell. Sur. Sanford Ransdell. Wit. James Taylor, Jr. Married 17 January by Rev. Nathaniel Sanders. p 29

16 November 1805. William FORD and Susanna Stubbling. Sur. James Lanton. p 67

6 December 1790. Benjamin FORTSON and Sally Head, dau. James Head, who consents. Sur. Shelton White. Wit. Henry Head. p 27

4 April 1776. Anthony FOSTER and Elizabeth Price. Found in Deed Book 17. Both of St. Thomas' Parish. Notation: by Banns. p 6

28 July 1794. Haskew FOSTER and Caty Snell. Sur. John Williams. Married 21 August by Rev. George Martin. p 35

11 October 1793. John FOSTER and Susannah Deering, dau. Robert Deering, who consents. Sur. John Williams. Wit. James Taylor. Married 15 October by Rev. George Eve. p 34

8 October 1774. Thomas FOSTER and Mary Sawyer. Found in Deed Book 17. Both of St. Thomas' Parish. Notation: by Banns. p 3

25 February 1777. Thomas FOSTER and Frances Jones. Found in Deed Book 17. Both of St. Thomas' Parish. Notation: by Banns. p 5

19 April 1793. William FOSTER and Tabitha Hawkins, who writes her own consent. Sur. Richard Hoard. Wit. Richard Graves. p 32

23 July 1791. Thornton FOUSHEE and Nancy Graves, dau. Richard Graves, who consents. Sur. John Graves. Married 28 July by Rev. Nathaniel Sanders. p 28

7 March 1796. Stephen FOX and Elizabeth Herndon. Sur. Zachariah Herndon, Jr. p 39

11 March 1785. John FRANKLYN and Mary Pearson, who writes her own consent. Sur. William Milligan. Wit. Lewis Franklin and John Reed. p 15

31 July 1790. Jonathan FRANKLYN and Susannah Breeding, dau. Job Breeding, who consents. Sur. Richard Breeding. Wit. Ephraim Breeding. Double Wedding! See Richard Breeding. p 26

4 June 1807. Shadrack FRAZIER and Polly Morris, dau. William Morris, who consents. Sur. James Morris. Wit. Elis Morris. Married 9 June by Rev. George Bingham. p 71

24 November 1808. Philip FREDERICK and Betsy Baugher. Married by Rev. George Bingham. p 73

2 June 1808. John FRYE and Catherine Baugher. Married by Rev. George Bingham. p 73

24 January 1773. John FURNACE and Elizabeth Duncome. Found in Deed Book 17. Both of St. Thomas' Parish. p 203

5 December 1782. Jacob FURNIS and Mary Page, dau. John Page, who consents. Sur. William Glass. Wit. James Furnis and John Ranes. Both of St. Thomas' Parish. p 11

29 September 1804. Augustine GAINES and Polly White. Sur. John White, who makes oath Polly is over 21; no relationship stated. Married 30 September by Rev. Hamilton Goss. p 64

21 July 1776. Francis GAINES and Betsy Lewis. Found in Deed Book 17. Both in St. Thomas Parish. Notation: by Banns. p 6

13 March 1793. John GAINES and Jenny Gaines. Sur. Richard Collins. Wit. Richard Gaines and Lovell Dogan. Edward Herndon, guardian of Jenny consents for her. p 32

5 March 1800. John GAINES and Joanna Sanders, dau. Nathaniel Sanders, who consents. Sur. George Mason. Wit. Benjamin Sanders and Reynolds Chapman. Married by Rev. Nathaniel Sanders. p 51

6 February 1782. Richard GAINES and Elizabeth Eastin, dau. Elizabeth Eastin who consents. Sur. Philip Eastin. Wit. Richard Gaines, Jr. Both of St. Thomas' Parish. p 11

26 December 1800. Thomas GAINES and Milley Row, dau. Thomas Row, who consents. Sur. William Row. Wit. Keeling Row and Reynolds Chapman. p 53

14 September 1795. John GALASBY and Betsy Goodridge, who writes her own consent. Sur. Richard Goodridge. Wit. James Taylor. p 37

1 January 1796. Matthew GAMBLE and Nancy Bell. Sur. David Holmes. Wit. James Taylor, Jr. p 39

23 December 1796. Samuel GAMBOE and Chatherine Chisham, dau. John Chisham, who consents. Sur. John Dawson. Wit. James Taylor, Jr. p 41

27 May 1801. Walter GAMBREL and Betsy Lee. Sur. William Lee. Wit. Reynolds Chapman. p 54

3 November 1795. William GARDE and Mary Yates, widow. Sur. Edward Bracken. p 38

19 November 1808. Andrew GARNETT and Sally B. Bell. Sur. William Bell, who makes oath both are over 21; no relationship stated. p 73

7 October 1807. James GARNETT and Frances Chiles, dau. James Chiles, who consents, is surety and makes oath James Garnett is over 21. Married 23 December by Rev. Robert Jones. p 71

22 December 1802. Larkin GARNETT and Elizabeth Bell, dau. Joseph and Elizabeth Bell, who consent. Sur. Roger Bell. Wit. John Bell and Patrick Bell. p 58

3 October 1760. Thomas GARNETT and Rachel Hawkins. This license found in an old fee book by J. W. Browning. Both of St. Thomas' Parish. p 1

15 November 1780. Thomas GARNETT and Suckey Brockman. Sur. Adam Lindsay. Wit. William Brockman. Samuel Brockman consents for Suckey (Susanna); no relationship stated. Both of St. Thomas' Parish. p 9

27 December 1788. Demey GARRETT and Sally Stanton, dau. Christy Stanton (mother), who consents. Sur. James Taylor. Wit. John Garrett and William Taylor. Married 18 January 1789 by Rev. George Eve. p 23

15 February 1798. Spencer GARTON and Polly Hancock, dau. William Hancock, who consents. Sur. James Taylor. Wit. Sally Hancock and Nelly Hancock. p 45

19 January 1773. Zachariah GARTON and Milley Sulling. Found in Deed Book 17. Both of St. Thomas' Parish. p 203

10 August 1805. Henry GATEWOOD and Amy Quisenberry, dau. Moses Quisenberry, deceased. Sur. Moses Quisenberry, who makes oath Amy is over 21. Her brother? p 66

9 March 1773. John GAYDEN and Catey Collins. Found in Deed Book 17. Both of St. Thomas' Parish. p 203

27 October 1800. Joshua GEAR and Jane Watson, dau. Isaac Watson, who consents. Sur. James Watson. Wit. John Dunnavin (or Dunnivan). p 52

21 August 1792. William GEAR and Sally Ham, granddau. Samuel Ham, who consents. Sur. James Haney. Wit. Joshua Gear and John Donoven. p 30

15 August 1798. William GEAR and Polly Rogers, dau. John Rogers, who consents. Sur. John Rogers, Jr. Wit. Ransom Gear. Married 21 August by Rev. George Bingham. p 46

28 January 1802. Jonathan GEER and Sarah Thrackwell. Married by Rev. George Bingham. p 56

23 February 1802. Ransom GEER and Polly Lamb. Married by Rev. George Bingham. p 57

18 November 1801. Aaron GENTRY and Polly Ogg. Married by Rev. George Bingham. p 55

- - 1771-74. - GEORGE and Catherine Spencer. (Supposed to be Isaac George.) This marriage found on a flyleaf of an old memorandum book in Orange County Court House by J. W. Browning. p 17

21 December 1803. John GEORGE and Elizabeth Long. Sur. William Long, who makes oath Elizabeth is over 21; no relationship stated. Married by Rev. Nathaniel Sanders, Baptist. p 62

13 February 1793. William GEORGE and Lucy Hawkins. Thomas Coleman, guardian of Lucy, consents for her. Wit. Edward George and Susanna Coleman. William Pannill, guardian of William George, consents for him. Wit. Edward George and Thomas Coleman. Sur. Edward George. p 31

16 August 1808. Thomas GIBBENS and Lucy Debord. Married by Rev. George Bingham. p 73

- - -. James GIBBS and Ann Johnson, widow. This marriage found on a flyleaf of an old memorandum book in Orange County Court House by J. W. Browning. p 17

27 December 1779. Julius GIBBS and Aggy Davis, dau. Joseph Davis, who consents. Sur. James Davis. Wit. Zachariah Gibbs and William Davis. Both of St. Thomas' Parish. p 9

14 February 1805. Zachariah GIBBS and Lucy Wayt, dau. James Wayt, who consents. Sur. William Wayt. Wit. James Burton. p 66

23 December 1809. Peter GIBSON and Fanny Estes. Sur. William Estes, who makes oath Fanny is over 21; no relationship stated. p 77

7 August 1798. John GIBSON and Elizabeth Harvey. Married by Rev. George Bingham. p 46

28 March 1803. William GIBSON and Betsy Cartey. Sur. Benjamin Hawley. p 60

17 May 1809. Aquila GILBERT and Fanny Newman. Sur. Thomas Newman, who makes oath Fanny is over 21; no relationship stated. Married by Rev. Robert Jones. p 75

11 May 1778. Thomas GILBERT and Anne Fearneaugh, dau. Thomas Fearneaugh, who consents. Sur. James Taylor, Jr. Wit. William Fearneaugh and John Terrill. Both in St. Thomas' Parish. p 8

7 June 1796. John GILLASPY and Ann White, dau. John White, Sr., who consents. Sur. Benjamin Cave, Jr. (her brother-in-law). p 40

3 June 1790. Sam'll GILLETT and Sally Pannill. Married by Rev. John Leland. p 26

7 January 1778. John GILLOCK and Hannah Wolfengerger. Found in Deed Book 17. Both in St. Thomas' Parish. p 7

26 May 1788. Lawrence GILLOCK and Betsy Twentyman. Sur. John Orant. p 22

8 January 1784. Thomas GILLOCK and Elizabeth Morgan. Sur. Joseph Thomas. In St. Thomas' Parish. p 13

27 June 1808. John GILMER and Sarah Minor. Sur. Dabney Minor. Married 28 June by Rev. Robert Jones. p 73

21 October 1776. Andrew GLASSELL and Elizabeth Taylor. Found in Deed Book 17. Both of St. Thomas' Parish. p 7

9 September 1788. Thomas GOFORTH and Milly Foster. Sur. John Foster. p 22

3 May 1798. Richard GOLDEN and Ann Walton. Richard son of William Golden. Married by Rev. George Bingham. p 46

28 July 1804. Reubin GOLDING and Polly Price, dau. George Price. Sur. John Price. Wit. Manuel Price. p 63

8 April 1793. David GOODALL and Elizabeth Davis, dau. Joseph Davis, who consents. Sur. John Davis. Wit. Reubin Smith. Married 10 April by Rev. George Eve. p 32

21 February 1809. David GOODALL and Tabitha Clark. Married by Rev. George Bingham. p 75

18 January 1808. Isaac GOODALL and Milly Huckstep. Sur. John Huckstep. Married 20 January by Rev. Jacob Watts. p 72

23 January 1782. James GOODALL and Sally Harvey. Both of St. Thomas' Parish. Sur. John Bell. p 11

19 December 1798. Jonathan GOODALL and Patsy Russell. Sur. Caleb Smoot. Married 23 December by Rev. George Bingham. p 47

20 December 1804. John GOODALL and Sally Davis. Married by Rev. George Bingham. p 65

9 February 1788. Parks GOODALL and Franky Cox. Sur. Thomas Cos. Wit. James Taylor. Married 14 February by Rev. George Eve. p 21

15 March 1785. William GOODALL and Lucy Davis, dau. Jonathan Davis, who consents. Sur. John Davis. Wit. Francis Taylor. p 15

14 March 1775. John GOODRICH and Betty Dear. Found in Deed Book 17. Both of St. Thomas' Parish. Notation: by Banns. p 3

25 March 1809. George C. GOODRIDGE and Fanny Burton, who writes her own consent. Sur. John Lucas. Wit. Milly Goodridge. Married 26 March by Rev. Jacob White. p 75

18 October 1785. Nathaniel GORDON and Mary Gordon, spinster. Sur. David Henning. p 16

9 December 1793. John GORE, Jr. and Gracey Grace, dau. George Grace, who consents. Sur. Joseph Booth. Wit. William Burton. Married 11 December by Rev. James Garnett. p 34

19 April 1809. Reubin GOSNEY and Elizabeth McKinney. Sur. William McKinney; no relationship stated. p 66

24 December 1798. Hamilton GOSS and Martha Major, widow. Sur. John Goss. p 47

9 January 1774. George GRACE and Anne McNeal. Found in Deed Book 17. Notation: by Banns. Both of St. Thomas' Parish. p 2

1 January 1800. Benjamin GRADY and Catherine Adams, who writes her own consent saying she is 20 years of age. Sur. John Montague. Wit. Reynolds Chapman. p 50

8 December 1807. John GRADY and Sarah Proctor, dau. John Proctor, who consents. Sur. George Proctor, Jr. Wit. John Proctor, Jr. Married 18 December by Rev. Nathaniel Sanders, Baptist. p 72

24 October 1801. Richmond GRADY and Hannah Montague. Sur. John Montague, who makes oath Hannah is over 21; no relationship stated. Married 25 October by Rev. Jeremiah Chandler. p 55

27 August 1801. Samuel GRADY and Caty Montague. Sur. John Henderson, who makes oath that Caty is over 21. Married 29 August by Rev. Duke W. Hullum. p 54

21 September 1804. Jesse GRANT and Sally Faulconer, dau. John Faulconer, who consents. Sur. Rebuin Faulconer. Wit. Peter Perry and John Faulconer, Jr. p 64

22 July 1784. Samuel GRANT and Lidia Craig. Sur. Elijah Craig. In St. Thomas' Parish. p 14

22 December 1809. George GRASTY and Elizabeth Payne, dau. John Payne, who consents. Sur. John G. Wright. Wit. Richard Hoard. p 77

26 March 1804. Goodrich Lightfoot GRASTY and Elizabeth Morton, widow, who writes her own consent. Sur. Thomas Coleman. p 63

19 December 1789. Absalom GRAVES and Felicia White, dau. John White, who consents. Sur. William White. Wit. James White. p 25

13 September 1796. Benjamin GRAVES and Elizabeth Collins, dau. William Collins, who consents. Sur. George Collins. p 41

22 September 1800. Jacob GRAVES and Fanny White. Sur. John White, who makes oath Fanny is 21 years of age. Wit. Reynolds Chapman. Married 8 October by Rev. Jacob Watts. p 52

20 December 1794. Joel GRAVES and Sarah Graves, spinster. Sur. Isaac Graves. p 36

24 November 1800. Roda GRAVES and Marian Marquess, dau. John Marquess, who consents. Sur. Moses Robinson. Wit. Thomas Bohannon. p 52

18 June 1788. Thomas GRAVES and Anna Grady, dau. William Grady, who consents. Sur. Lincfield Grady. Wit. George Gordon and William B. Webb. p 22

5 February 1791. Thomas GRAVES, Jr. and Mourning Burroughs, dau. Frances Burrus, who consents. Sur. Christopher Dickin. Wit. Isaac Graves. (Mourning, dau. Thomas Burrus and Frances Tandy. Thomas Graves, Jr. son of Thomas Graves and Sarah Delaney. 14 T 119.) p 27

12 June 1805. Waller GRAVES and Polly Rucker, dau. Mary Rucker. Sur. William Rucker. Wit. Nancy Rucker. p 66

22 December 1796. William GRAVES and Betsy Hilman. Sur. Uriel Hilman. p 41

9 February 1804. William GRAVES and Peggy White, dau. John White.
Sur. Benjamin Cave, Jr. Wit. Augustine Gaines. Married by Rev.
Hamilton Goss. p 62

6 January 1757. Nicholas GREEN and Elizabeth Price. This license found
in an old fee book by J. W. Browning. Both of St. Thomas' Parish.
p 1

23 September 1793. Abell GRIFFEY and Catherine Sutton. Sur. William
Sutton. Wit. James Taylor, Jr. p 33

15 October 1789. Joseph GRIFFEY and Fanny Wisdom, spinster. Sur.
Edmund Burrus. Wit. James Taylor. p 24

23 May 1796. Elisha GRIGSBY and Elizabeth Porter, dau. Abner Porter,
who consents. Sur. John Porter. Wit. John Pendleton. Married
27 May by Rev. George Eve. p 40

22 January 1798. John GROOM and Dise Delaney, who gives her own consent,
witnessed by Major Groom and Richard B. Webb. Sur. Jacob Williams.
Wit. James Taylor, Jr. p 45

22 March 1781. John GULLEY and Mary Land, dau. John Land, who consents.
Sur. Enoch Gulley. Wit. Stephen Eastin. Mary in bond; Elizabeth
in consent. p 10

27 December 1807. Ambrose HALL and Elizabeth Marr. Married by Rev.
George Bingham. p 72

2 December 1802. Bazel HALL and Docia Maiden. Married by Rev. George
Bingham. p 58

2 January 1800. William HALL and Susannah Davis. Married by Rev.
George Bingham. p 50

18 June 1801. William J. HALL and Elizabeth Bell Shepherd, dau. Andrew
Shepherd, who consents. Sur. William Shepherd. Wit. Reynolds Chapman. p 54

12 December 1783. Joseph HAM and Sarah Hearen. Sur. William Glass.
Wit. Samuel Ham, James Head and Anthony Foster. Frances and Sarah
Hearen consent for Sarah; no relationship stated. p 13

5 March 1804. Joseph HAM and Nancy Smoot. Sur. Caleb Smoot, who makes
oath Nancy is over 21; no relationship stated. p 62

18 January 1773. Samuel HAM and Clary Wisdom. Found in Deed Book 17.
Both of St. Thomas' Parish. p 203

9 August 1793. Edward HAMBLETON and Elizabeth Rippito. John Rippito
consents for Elizabeth; no relationship stated. Sur. William
Rippito. Wit. Peter Rippito and Thaddeus Blackey. p 33

28 December 1802. Elige HAMBLETON and Polly Bayle, under age, dau. John Bayle, who consents. Sur. Alford Battle. Wit. William Brook. Married 30 December by Rev. Nathaniel Sanders, Baptist. p 59

12 January 1800. LeRoy HAMBLETON and Suckey Blunt, dau. Michael Blunt, who consents. Sur. John Finnell. Wit. Macon Biggers. Married by Rev. James Garnett. p 50

23 March 1796. Theophilus HAMBLETON and Nutty Powell. Sur. John Hambleton. Married 25 March by Rev. Nathaniel Sanders. p 39

23 June 1803. Thomas HAMBLETON and Margaret Coleman, dau. John Coleman, who consents, and is surety. p 60

23 December 1788. John HAMILTON and Frances Richards, dau. William Richards, who consents. Sur. James Jones. Wit. Ambrose Richards. Married 24 December by Rev. John Leland. p 23

25 August 1801. John HAMILTON and Sarah W. Rippetoe. Edward Hambleton, guardian of Sarah, consents for her and is surety. Married 27 August by Rev. Hamilton Goss. p 54

24 December 1799. William HAMILTON and Jensey Olive, dau. Elizabeth Olive, who consents. Sur. Francis Jones. Wit. Thomas Olive, who makes oath both are of full age. p 50

10 October 1805. James HANCOCK and Elender Hancock, dau. William Hancock, who consents. Sur. William Armstrong. Wit. Edward Harris. Married 11 October by Rev. Robert Jones. p 67

4 May 1775. William HANCOCK and Jemima Brock. Found in Deed Book 17. Notation: by Banns. William of Trinity Parish; Jemima of St. Thomas' Parish. p 3

1 May 1784. James HANEY and Nancy Petros, dau. Matthew and Jane Petros, who consent. Sur. John Goodall. Wit. Edmund Shackelford. p 13

23 December 1805. James HARRIS and Sally Estes. Sur. William Estes, who makes oath Sally is over 21; no relationship stated. Married 25 December by Rev. George Bingham. p 67

17 November 1774. John HARRIS and Frances Rowzee. Found in Deed Book 17. Both of St. Thomas' Parish. p 3

3 November 1800. John HARRIS and Milly Price, widow. Sur. Thomas Bell. Wit. Reynolds Chapman. p 52

3 May 1806. Lewis HARRISON and Nancy Harrison. Married by Rev. William Douglass, Methodist. p 68

27 February 1797. Peter HARRIS and Mary Stanfield Estes. Sur. William Estes. p 43

20 April 1796. Benjamin HARROD and Elizabeth Blair, dau. Betsy Blair, who consents. Sur. Absalom Tyler. p 40

3 August 1803. Richard HARROD and Joanna Arnold, dau. Willis Arnold, who consents and is surety. Married by Rev. William Calhoun. p 61

22 February 1808. Anthony HARVEY and Polly Bingham, dau. George Bingham, who consents. Sur. Richard Golding. Wit. Reuben Golding, Thomas Foster and Josias Bingham. p 72

23 February 1775. Benjamin HARVEY and Susanna Harvey. Found in Deed Book 17. Both of St. Thomas' Parish. Notation: by Banns. p 3

19 April 1778. John HARVEY and Lucy Estes. Found in Deed Book 17. Both of St. Thomas' Parish. Notation: by Banns. p 8

22 January 1800. John HARVEY and Elizabeth Felix, dau. William Felix, who consents. Sur. William Bradley. Wit. James Gillum. Married by Rev. Hamilton Goss. p 50

19 April 1778. Thomas HARVEY and Sarah Hobbs. Found in Deed Book 17. Both of St. Thomas' Parish. Notation: by Banns. p 8

12 July 1800. William HARVEY and Alley Wood, dau. Hopeful Wood, who consents. Sur. Charles Coppedge. Wit. John Harvey and Reynolds Chapman. p 51

16 March 1802. Jonathan HARVY and Margaret Ross. Married by Rev. George Bingham. p 57

7 March 1791. Moses HARWOOD and Elizabeth Sutton, who writes her own consent. Sur. William Sutton. p 27

2 April 1796. Conrad HAUSE, Jr. and Susannah Thompson. Sur. Conrad Hause, Sr. Wit. James Taylor, Jr. p 39

15 October 1807. Alexander HAWKINS and Anna Scott. Sur. George Scott, who makes oath both are over 21; no relationship stated. Married 17 October by Rev. Nathaniel Sanders, Baptist. p 71

1 March 1799. Benjamin HAWKINS and Sally Scott, spinster. Sur. Reuben Scott. Married 7 March by Rev. Nathaniel Sanders. p 48

16 March 1802. Benjamin HAWKINS and Polly Bickers. Sur. Nicholas Bickers. Married by Rev. Frederick Kabler, Lutheran. p 57

8 January 1807. Elijah HAWKINS and Elizabeth Scott. Sur. George Scott, who makes oath both are over 21; no relationship stated. Wit. John Allen. Married by Rev. Nathaniel Sanders, Baptist. p 70

3 September 1799. James HAWKINS and Betsy Coleman, dau. James Coleman, who consents. Sur. Joseph Bledsoe. Wit. Reuben Scott. p 49

11 November 1799. James HAWKINS and Elizabeth Rector. Sur. Ikey Richards. Wit. John Robinson and Reynolds Chapman. Written I Key Richards in another place. p 49

28 October 1780. Jehu HAWKINS and Mary Gaines, widow. Both of St. Thomas' Parish. Sur. John Hawkins and Areulues Hawkins. p 9

3 March 1770. Moses HAWKINS and Susanna Strother. Both of St. Thomas' Parish. This marriage found in an old fee book by J. W. Browning. p 2

23 April 1804. Moses HAWKINS and Joice Quisenberry. Sur. Moses Quisenberry. p 63

26 March 1803. Roddy HAWKINS and Alice Chamberlane. Sur. Richard Gaines. Wit. Elizabeth Wall Hawkins. Roddy, son of Reuben Hawkins, who consents. Married 31 March by Rev. Nathaniel Sanders, Baptist. p 60

14 September 1803. Benjamin HAWLEY and Frances Edwards. Sur. Joseph Edwards, who makes oath Frances is over 21; no relationship stated. Married 15 September by Rev. Robert Jones. p 61

28 October 1780. Moses HAYES and Sarah Petty, spinster. Both of St. Thomas' Parish. Sur. Joseph Hawkins. p 9

21 August 1784. Benjamin HEAD, Jr. and Margaret Gaar, dau. Lewis Gaar, who consents. Sur. William Head. Wit. Capt. May Burton, Jr. In St. Thomas' Parish. p 14

11 November 1789. George Marshall HEAD and Milley Rucker, dau. John and Mary Rucker, who consent. Sur. Joel Rucker. Wit. Capt. May Burton, Jr. p 24

5 November 1794. Henry HEAD and Elizabeth Sanford, dau. Ann Sanford, who consents. Sur. Durrett Sanford. Wit. Augustine Sanford. p 35

5 December 1775. James HEAD and Elizabeth Jannet Kirtley. Found in Deed Book 17. Notation: by Banns. Elizabeth of Brumfield Parish; James of St. Thomas' Parish. p 4

26 November 1787. John HEAD and Nancy Sanford, dau. Ann Sanford, who consents. Sur. Richard Sanford. Wit. James Head. p 20

20 December 1798. Tavenah HEAD and Jenney Plunkett, dau. Jesse Plunkett, who consents. Sur. John Plunkett. p 47

31 May 1784. William HELM and Matilda Taliaferro, under age, dau. Francis Taliaferro, who consents. Sur. Hay Taliaferro. Wit. William Edwards. Both of St. Thomas' Parish. p 14

16 April 1810. Ambrose HENDERSON and Lucy Acree, dau. William Acree, who is surety. Married by Rev. Ambrose Brockman of Albemarle County. p 78

2 January 1798. John HENDERSON and Frankey Daniel. Sur. Caleb Lindsay. Wit. James Taylor. p 45

24 November 1804. Ogborne HENLEY and Martha Winslow, dau. Benjamin Winslow, who consents. Sur. Edward Winslow. Wit. James Madison. Married 25 November by Rev. Robert Jones. p 64

25 November 1793. Peter HENNESSY and Winney Routt, widow. Sur. James Taylor. Wit. William Goodridge. Peter Hennessy of Albermarle County. p 34

13 February 1802. Belfield HENRY and Elizabeth Kirtley. Married by Rev. George Bingham. p 56

12 May 1792. Benjamin HENRY and Nancy Roberts, dau. Hugh Roberts, who consents. Sur. Thomas Roberts. Married by Rev. George Eve. p 30

22 April 1793. William HENRY and Elizabeth Warren, widow. Sur. Thomas Roberts. Married 25 April by Rev. George Eve. p 32

17 November 1801. Zachary HENRY and Lucy Kirtley. Married by Rev. George Bingham. p 55

22 September 1785. Edmund HENSHOW and Mary Newman, dau. James Newman, who consents. Sur. James Newman, Jr. Wit. Thomas Newman. p 16

4 December 1780. John HENSHAW and Patty Newman, dau. James Newman, who consents. Sur. William Newman. Both of St. Thomas' Parish. p 10

20 August 1792. John HENSHAW and Elizabeth Newman, dau. James and Elizabeth Newman, who consent. Sur. Thomas Newman. Wit. James Taylor, Jr. p 30

18 September 1809. Cypress HENSLEY and Caty Thompson. Sur. John Thompson, who makes oath Caty is over 21; no relationship stated. Married 24 September by Rev. Jacob Watts. p 76

23 December 1802. James HENSLEY and Elizabeth Maiden. Married by Rev. George Bingham. p 58

16 January 1808. Jeder HENSLEY and Winney Thompson, dau. George
Thompson, who consents. Sur. Armistead Brown. Wit. Cyprus Hensley.
Married 21 January by Rev. Jacob Watts. p 72

8 December 1810. John HENSLEY and Elizabeth Oliver, dau. Francis Oliver,
who is surety and makes oath John Hensley is over 21. Married by
Rev. Ambrose Brockman of Albemarle County. p 79

28 October 1785. Lewis HENSLEY and Mary Foster. Sur. Eastham Snell.
p 16

4 January 1810. Frederick HERMAN and Mary Jamason, widow, who writes
her own consent. Sur. Philemon Davis. Married by Rev. Robert Jones.
p 77

20 November 1787. Benjamin HERNDON and Catherine Ehart. Married by
Rev. George Eve. (John Goodwin Herndon in his "William Herndon of
Orange County" p 151 says this is an error. It should be Susanna
Ehart. Benjamin b. 9 May 1765 d. 12 April 1805. Susanna Ahart
Herndon b. 8 July 1769, d. 12 June 1835 administered his estate.) p 20

9 October 1805. Benjamin HERNDON and Mary Stephens, dau. Benjamin
Stephens, who consents. Sur. Thomas Herndon. Wit. William Nelson
and John Stephens. Married by Rev. Robert Jones. p 67

26 March 1806. George HERNDON and Sarah Teale, dau. Henry Teale. Sur.
Henry Teale and Benjamin P. Gaines. Wit. Richard M. Chapman.
Married 1 April by Rev. Nathaniel Sanders. p 68

11 December 1802. Henry HERNDON and Lucinda Wood, dau. James Wood, who
consents. Sur. Robert Reynolds. Wit. John Wood. Married 16
December by Rev. Hamilton Goss. Henry Herndon of Madison County,
son of Edward and Mary (Gaines) Herndon. p 58

19 April 1781. John HERNDON and Elizabeth Wrights, dau. John Wright, who
consents. Sur. William Wright. Married 25 April by Rev. Nathaniel
Sanders. p 10

15 December 1809. John HERNDON and Nancy Adams, dau. William Adams, who
is surety; also makes oath John is over 21. p 77

5 May 1787. William HERNDON and Sukey Perry. Sur. Moses Bledsoe. p 19

- - 1771. Zachariah HERNDON and Mary Scott. This marriage found on a
flyleaf of a memorandum book in Orange County Court House by J. W.
Browning. p 17

2 April 1784. James HERRING and Judah Cofer, dau. James Cofer, who
consents. Sur. Peter Rucker. Wit. James and Mary Beazley. In
St. Thomas' Parish. p 13

7 February 1788. William HERRING and Molly Shiflett, dau. William
Shiflett, who consents. Sur. Richard Williams. Married by Rev.
George Eve. p 21

4 November 1799. John HESTAND and Zantipy Newell. Sur. Abraham Hestand.
Wit. Reynolds Chapman. p 49

27 May 1784. Jonathan HIATT and Mary Connor, dau. Rachel Connor, who
consents. Sur. Lewis Connor. Wit. John Connor. Both in St. Thomas'
Parish. p 14

13 January 1809. Charles HICKS and Judith Watson. Married by Rev.
George Bingham. p 74

3 June 1796. John HIGDON and Mary Ross. Married by Rev. George
Bingham. p 40

30 December 1783. John HIEATT and Sarah Arnold. Sur. Nicholas Arnold.
In St. Thomas' Parish. p 13

24 December 1783. Lewis HIEATT and Barbary Allen, spinster. Sur.
Thomas Davis. In St. Thomas' Parish. p 13

4 February 1806. Jacob HIGHLANDER and Fanny Pettis, dau. John Pettis.
Sur. William Loyd. Wit. Spencer R. Pettis and Edmund B. Pettis,
brothers of Fanny. p 68

5 March 1778. Henry HILL and Susanna Jones. Found in Deed Book 17.
Both of St. Thomas' Parish. p 8

24 December 1788. Samuel HILL and Nancy Tate. Sur. Uriah Tate.
Wit. James Taylor. p 23

26 August 1805. Joseph HILMAN and Susanna Abell, dau. Caleb Abell, who
is surety. Married 11 September by Rev. Ephraim Abell. p 66

11 July 1797. Uriel HILMAN and Sally Graves. Sur. Thomas Graves.
Wit. James Taylor. p 43

31 December 1782. Maj. Isaac HITE, Jr. and Nellie Madison, born
14 February 1760, dau. Col. James and Eleanor (Conway) Madison, who
were married 13 September 1749. Sur. Ambrose Madison (brother).
Both of St. Thomas' Parish. p 11

28 November 1803. Isaac HITE and Ann Tunstall Maury. Sur. Leonard Hill
Maury, who makes oath Ann is over 21; no relationship stated. p 61

28 October 1810. Washington HOARD and Elizabeth Adams. Sur. George
Perry. Wit. Simon Perry. Washington, son of Richard Hoard, who
consents. Married by Rev. Jeremiah Chandler. p 79

16 August 1790. John HOBDAY and Mary Davis. Married by Rev. Nathaniel Sanders. p 26

21 March 1757. George HOLLAND and Mary Coleman. This license found in an old fee book by J. W. Browning. Both of St. Thomas' Parish. p 1

25 July 1803. George HOLSAPPLE and Pheby Hubbert, dau. Peter Hubert. Sur. Jacob Holsapple. p 60

22 December 1795. Joseph HOMES and Sally Hilman, age 23, dau. Joseph Hilman, who consents. Sur. William Graves. Wit. James Taylor. Probably Holmes. p 38

4 August 1809. James HORSLEY and Jane Chiles, dau. James Chiles, who is surety. p 76

11 March 1793. Charles P. HOWARD and Jane Taylor. Sur. Charles Wardell. p 32

28 December 1790. Richard HOWARD and Margaret Sullivan. Sur. William Faulconer. Wit. James Taylor. p 27

16 January 1793. Carter HUBBARD and Betsey Durrett. Sur. Joel Durrett. Wit. James Taylor. p 31

26 December 1804. Joseph HUBBARD and Diana Durrett, dau. Joel Durrett. Sur. Larkin Durrett. Wit. Carter Hubbard. Married by Rev. Robert Jones. p 65

2 April 1793. John HUDSON and Mary Dedman. Sur. Francis Taylor. Wit. James Taylor. p 32

3 December 1803. Alexander HUGHES and Elizabeth Mitchell, dau. Wiat Mitchell, who consents. Sur. Marmaduke Branham. Wit. Francis Hughes. Married 22 December by Rev. Nathaniel Sanders, Baptist. p 61

23 April 1800. Armstead HUGHES and Sally Chisham, dau. John Chisham, who consents. Sur. William Dawson. Wit. John Dawson and Reynolds Chapman. Married 27 April by Rev. Hamilton Goss. p 51

8 June 1775. Thomas HUGHES and Mary Davis. Found in Deed Book 17. Both of St. Thomas' Parish. p 3

9 June 1808. William HUMBLE and Mary Overton, dau. Willis Overton, who consents. Sur. Eliphelet Johnson. Wit. Hackley Warren and George Overton. p 73

25 August 1801. Benjamin HUME and Elizabeth Taliaferro, widow of Col. William Taliaferro. Sur. William W. Hume. Married by Rev. Frederick Kabler, Lutheran. p 54

30 January 1801. Francis HUMES and Ellizabeth Pain, dau. Reuben Pain, who consents. Sur. William Foster. Wit. Charles Pain. p 53

26 November 1774. William HUMPHRIES and Susanna Webb. Found in Deed Book 17. Notation: by Banns. Both of St. Thomas' Parish. p 3

23 January 1797. James HUNDLEY and Susanna Chiles. Sur. Benjamin Cave. p 42

12 July 1794. John HUNDLEY and Nancy Loyd. Sur. Nehemiah Hundley. p 35

9 February 1798. Joshua HUNDLEY and Betsy Gressom, spinster. Sur. James Hundley. Wit. James Taylor. p 45

4 August 1790. Nehemiah HUNDLEY and Elizabeth Cave. Benjamin Cave consents for Elizabeth; no relationship stated. Sur. Coalby Smith. Wit. Elizabeth Cave. p 26

23 August 1802. James HUNT and Susannah Darnold. Sur. Abraham Darnold, who makes oath Susannah is over 21. Married 26 August by Rev. Hamilton Goss. p 58

9 December 1808. Robert HUNT and Frances Darnell, dau. Mary Ann Darnell, who signs consent. Sur. James Hunt. Wit. Nancy Darnell. p 74

25 November 1799. Pleasant HUNTER and Jane Harris, dau. Lindsay Harris, who consents and is surety. Wit. Reynolds Chapman. p 49

8 October 1800. James HUTCHERSON and Catharine Deare, dau. Thomas Deare, who consents. Sur. James Johnston. Wit. Robert Rucker. p 52

23 March 1795. William HUTCHISON and Siler Robinson, dau. John Robinson, who consents. Sur. William Robinson. Wit. Richard Robinson. p 36

15 December 1760. Jacob HYTE and Frances Beale. This license found in an old fee book by J. W. Browning. Both of St. Thomas' Parish. p 1

19 January 1809. John JACKSON and Mary (Polly) Herndon. Married by Rev. George Bingham. Mary, dau. of Edward and Mary Ann (Gaines) Herndon and granddau. of William Herndon and James and Mary Gaines. p 74

30 December 1799. Benjamin JACOBS and Sarah Martin, dau. Henry Martin, who consents. Sur. Matthew Bridges. Wit. George Martin and Robert True. Married 2 January 1800 by Rev. Nathaniel Sanders. p 50

19 December 1806. Nathan JACOBS and Nancy Straghan, born 14 May 1783; writes her own consent. Sur. Albin Elliott. Married by Rev. Nathaniel Sanders. p 69

21 August 1802. William JACOBS and Polly Martin, dau. Henry Martin, who consents. Sur. Benjamin Jacobs. Wit. George Martin. Married 24 August by Rev. Nathaniel Sanders, Baptist. p 57

6 April 1773. Daniel JAMES and Lucy Davis. Found in Deed Book 17. Lucy born in Culpeper County, now in St. Thomas' Parish. Daniel of St. Mark's Parish, Culpeper County. p 203

21 August 1780. Spencer JAMES and Frances Davis. Both of St. Thomas' Parish. Sur. Philemon Davis. p 9

12 December 1792. Thomas R. JAMESON and Polly Samuel, spinster. Sur. Henry Samuel. Wit. James Taylor. p 31

19 December 1797. Elisha JARRELL and Nancy Bradley. George Bradley consents for Nancy; no relationship stated. Sur. Samuel Smith. Wit. George McDaniel, Abram McDaniel, Charles Beazley and John Beazley. Married 21 December by Rev. Hamilton Goss. p 44

23 May 1793. James JARRELL and Frances Sims. Sur. Zachariah Taylor. Wit. James Taylor. Married 13 June by Rev. George Eve. James signs the bond as Gerrill. p 33

14 March 1797. James JARRELL and Sarah Taylor. Married by Rev. George Bingham. p 43

24 November 1797. Zachariah JARRELL and Fanny Sims, dau. William and Nancy Sims, who consent. Sur. Sanders Walker. Wit. John Booten and Charles Bell. p 44

26 November 1810. John JENKINS and Sarah Terry. Sur. Reubin Oakes, who makes oath Sarah is over 21. p 79

14 January 1800. Thomas JENKINS and Elizabeth G. Taylor. Sur. Charles Taylor. p 50

19 December 1808. William S. JENKINS and Sally Pettis, dau. John Pettess. Sur. Edmund B. Pettys. Wit. Spencer Pettis. p 74

5 June 1795. Isaac JOHNSON, Jr. and Elizabeth Terrill. Sur. Archibald Terrill. Wit. James Taylor. p 37

18 May 1801. James JOHNSTON and Elizabeth Smith, dau. Absalem Smith, who consents and is surety. p 53

21 May 1807. James JOHNSON and Nancy Quisenberry, of age, dau. Mary Quisenberry, who consents. Sur. Spencer Atkins. Wit. Henry Quisenberry. Married 22 May by Rev. Robert Jones. p 71

31 January 1773. Joseph Bain JOHNSON and Elizabeth Shropshire. Found in Deed Book 17. Both of St. Thomas' Parish. p 203

1 February 1809. Richard JOHNSON and Lucy Alcocke. Sur. Joseph Alcocke, who makes oath Lucy is over 21; no relationship stated. p 75

31 January 1797. Thomas JOHNSON and Diannah Richards, dau. William Richards, who consents. Sur. Philemon Richards. Wit. James Taylor. p 42

31 January 1791. Valentine JOHNSON and Nancy Bennett. Sur. Howard Bennett. Married 7 February by Rev. George Eve. This minister's return is on p 29. p 27

30 August 1803. Valentine JOHNSON and Elizabeth Cave, dau. Belfield Cave, who consents. Sur. Richard Cave. Wit. Benjamin Cave. p 61

10 February 1770. William JOHNSON and Anne Barnett. Both of St. Thomas' Parish. This marriage found in an old fee book by J. W. Browning. Both of St. Thomas' Parish. p 2

22 September 1802. William JOHNSON and Alice Fitzhugh. Sur. Henry Fitzhugh; no relationship stated. p 58

12 - 1774. Benjamin JONES and Elizabeth Foster. Found in Deed Book 17. Notation: by Banns. Both of St. Thomas' Parish. p 2

7 September 1785. James JONES and Caty Robinson, dau. John Robinson, who consents. Sur. John Jones. Wit. William Robinson and Arucules Hawkins. p 16

7 September 1785. John JONES and Margaret Abell, widow. Sur. James Jones. (Probably Margaret Tinder, widow of John Abel.) p 16

3 August 1789. Reuben JONES and Patty Stowers, spinster. Sur. Jeremiah Bryant, Jr. Mary Stowers consents for Patty; no relationship stated. p 24

10 March 1760. Richard JONES and Grace Leonard. This license found in an old fee book by J. W. Browning. Both of St. Thomas' Parish. p 1

3 June 1800. Rev. Robert JONES and Mary Herndon (widow); writes her own consent. Sur. Hamilton Goss. Wit. Reynolds Chapman. Married by Rev. Hamilton Goss. (I think she was Mary (Scott) Herndon, widow of Zachariah Herndon, Rev. Sol. who died in Oragne County 1796.) p 51

25 March 1802. Walter JONES and Sally Freeman. Married by Rev. George Bingham. p 57

15 November 1787. Zachariah JONES and Rebecca Deane. Sur. John Jones. p 20

11 March 1786. Jonathan JOSEPH and Sarah Deering. Sur. Thomas Deering. Wit. Robert Deering, Jr. Robert Deering, Sr. consents for Sarah; no relationship stated. p 18

7 January 1802. Nelson KEATON and Edna Davis. Married by Rev. George Bingham. p 56

19 February 1805. Spencer KELLY and Lianna Rumsey. Sur John Sleet, who makes oath Lianna is over 21. p 66

18 May 1803. Peyton KEITH and Sally Petty, dau. George Petty, who consents. Sur. Thomas Procter. Wit. Thomas Clark. Married by Rev. James Garnett. p 60

15 December 1796. Robert KINDELL and Ursula Garnett. Sur. Adam Lindsay. Wit. James Taylor, Jr. p 41

-    -   1780. Azariah KING and Mary Abell. Sur. Caleb Abell. Wit. William Wright and Richard Abell. p 10

6 December 1799. Gabriel KING and Hulday Biggers, dau. Macon Biggers, who consents. Sur. William Biggers. Wit. Reynolds Chapman and George C. Taylor. Married by Rev. James Garnett. p 49

3 July 1804. John KING and Cythnia Row, dau. Edmund Row. Sur. Abner Row. Wit. Thomas Row. Married by Rev. Nathaniel Sanders, Baptist. p 63

27 April 1807. John KING and Frances Yates. Sur. James Yates. Wit. Charles Yates; no relationship stated. John, son of Julian King, who consents for him. Married 28 April by Rev. Robert Jones. p 70

15 December 1785. Sadrut KING and Mary Wayt, dau. James Wayt, who consents. Sur. Richard White. Wit. William Wayt. p 16

20 December 1806. William KINNEY and Fanny Beale. Sur. Cornelius Devenney makes oath Fanny is over 21. Married by Rev. Robert Jones. p 69

13 October 1801. Jonathan KIRTLEY and Theodoshia Anderson. Married by Rev. George Bingham. p 54

20 November 1810. Joseph KIRTLEY and Elizabeth Sims, dau. Jeremiah Sims, who consents. Sur. Pemperton Sims. Wit. Henry F. Hume. Married 6 December by Rev. George Bingham. Could this be Pemberton Sims? p 79

16 November 1800. Sinclear KIRTLEY and Ann Pannill, dau. William
Pannill, who consents. Sur. Morton Pannill. Wit. William Morton.
This name also written St. Clair. p 52

31 December 1802. Willis KIRTLEY and Mary Presley Thornton, dau. George
Thornton, who consents. Sur. Peter Thornton. Wit. Edward Eastham.
Married 2 January 1803 by Rev. Jacob Watts. p 59

23 August 1781. William Butcher KNIGHT and Frances Cave. Sur. William
Cave. Wit. James Taylor, Jr. Married 25 August by Rev. George Eve.
p 28

23 February 1797. William KNIGHT and Delphia Oakes. Sur. Thomas Oakes.
p 43

29 January 1799. William KNIGHT and Elizabeth Rogers. Married by
Rev. George Bingham. p 48

17 January 1797. Benjamin LAMB and Peggy Lamb, dau. John Lamb, who
consents. Sur. John Lamb, Jr. Wit. James Taylor, Jr. Married
19 January by Rev. George Bingham. p 42

20 October 1791. James LAMB and Ann Watson, dau. Isaac Watson, who
consents. Sur. John Lamb, Jr., John Goodall, Jr. and John Lamb. p 29

13 February 1800. Jeremiah LAMB and Ann Jones. Married by Rev. George
Bingham. p 50

25 October 1784. John LAMB and Nelly Lamb, born 22 April 1764, dau.
John Lamb, who consents. Sur. Thomas Lamb. Wit. William Harvey.
p 14

6 April 1808. John LAMB and Polly Watson. Sur. Joshua Gear, who makes
oath both are over 21. Married 10 April by Rev. George Bingham.
p 73

23 December 1798. William LAMB and Mary Gear; writes her own consent.
Sur. John Murray. Wit. James Early. Married 27 December by Rev.
George Bingham. p 47

6 August 1804. William LAMB and Elizabeth Herring. Married by Rev.
George Bingham. p 63

30 September 1807. Willis LAMB and Rebecca Slaughter, dau. Ann Slaughter,
who consents. Willis son of William Lamb, Sr., who consents for him.
Sur. William B. Knight. Wit. Matthew Lamb. Married by Rev. George
Bingham. p 71

18 December 1804. Edmond LANCASTER and Sally Cooper, who signs her own
consent. Sur. William Robinson. Wit. Benjamin Cooper and Richard
Webb. p 65

26 July 1794. Henry LANCASTER and Mary Wright, who gives her own consent. Sur. George Finnell. Wit. James Taylor. p 35

2 June 1792. Reuben LANCASTER and Betsey Conner. Sur. John Conner. p 30

30 March 1777. Richard LANCASTER and Johanna Singleton. Found in Deed Book 17. Both in St. Thomas' Parish. Notation: by Banns. p 5

2 November 1780. Robert LANCASTER and Lucy Dear, dau. John Dear, who consents and is surety. Wit. Thomas Dear. Both of St. Thomas' Parish. p 9

16 November 1775. Thomas LANCASTER and Frances Nailey. Found in Deed Book 17. Both in St. Thomas' Parish. Notation: by Banns. p 4

27 October 1802. Reubin LANDRAM and Susannah Atkins, dau. John and Susannah Atkins, who consent. Sur. John Atkins. Wit. David Harris and Rebecca Atkins. p 58

7 February 1794. John LANDRUM and Mary Collins, dau. Edward Collins, who consents. Sur. Thomas Landrum. p 34

24 December 1802. Lewis LANDRUM and Rebecca Atkins, dau. John and Rebecca Atkins, who consent. Sur. John Atkins. Wit. William Bell and Lydia Atkins. Lewis, son of Reubin Landram, who consents for him. p 59

23 December 1798. John LANE and Tabitha Crew. Married by Rev. George Bingham. p 47

14 March 1803. Robert G. LANDE and Polly Whitelaw, dau. Thomas and Elizabeth Whitelaw. Sur. Ellis Hambleton. Wit. William Hambleton. Married 17 March by Rev. William Douglass, Methodist. p 60

28 August 1783. Thomas LANTON and Mary Walker. Married by Rev. Aaron Bledsoe. p 13

20 December 1787. Jacob LANTOR and Polly Webb. Sur. Henry Clayton. Wit. John Foster. p 20

31 May 1787. Peter LANTOR and Hannah Webb. Sur. Morton Jones. p 19

14 July 1777. Gidieon LEA and Anny Coffery. Found in Deed Book 17. Both in St. Thomas' Parish. Notation: by Banns. p 5

21 December 1784. Robert LEAK and Susanna Leak. Sur. Lewis Willis. In St. Thomas' Parish. p 14

4 March 1777. John LEATHERER and Sarah White. Found in Deed Book 17. Both of St. Thomas' Parish. Notation: by Banns. p 5

23 September 1807. Jonathan LEATHERS and Betsy Payne, dau. Thomas Payne. Sur. Elijah Mallory. Wit. Robert Payne. p 71

18 April 1792. William LEATHERS and Nancy Finnell. Sur. Roger Bell. Wit. James Taylor. p 30

28 January 1805. Lewis LEAVELL and Frances Bell, dau. John Bell, who consents. Sur. John W. Powell. Wit. James Haydon. Married by Rev. Hamilton Goss. p 65

6 January 1808. Abner LEE and Sally Lee. Sur. Samuel Lee, who makes oath Sally is over 21; no relationship stated. Married by Rev. Nathaniel Sanders. p 72

10 November 1800. George LEE and Caty Foster, dau. William Foster, who consents and is surety. Wit. Reynolds Chapman. p 52

18 December 1781. Major John LEE and Elizabeth Bell, dau. Thomas Bell, who consents. Sur. Ambrose Madison. Wit. Ann Bell. Both of St. Thomas' Parish. p 10

17 June 1785. Kendall LEE and Sarah Gordon. Sur. James Gordon, Jr. p 15

24 February 1789. Richard LEE and Anna Dodd. Sur. Mordecai Mastin. Wit. James Taylor. Married by Rev. John Leland. p 23

23 December 1799. William LEE and Polly Simeco, 21 years of age. Sur. John Simeco. Wit. Reynolds Chapman. p 50

25 May 1790. Zachary LEE and Sarah Mankspoil, dau. Adam and Mary Mankspoil, who consent. Sur. Abner Watson. Wit. James Taylor, Jr. p 26

20 August 1794. James LEWIS and Nancy Watkins, dau. Isham Watkins, who consents. Sur. James Landrum. Wit. Joel Watkins. p 35

9 March 1785. Caleb LINDSAY and Sally Stevens, dau. John Stevens, who consents and is surety. Wit. James Stevens, Jr., James Duncan and Francis Taylor. p 15

15 November 1808. Reuben LINDSAY and Fanny (Frances) Mills. Sur. Nathaniel Mills, Jr. (Mrs. Hiden says Frances Mills b. 27 August 1783, dau. of Nathaniel Mills, Sr. and his wife, Frances Thompson m. 22 October 1771. Reuben Lindsay, son of Adam Lindsay and his wife, Betty Garnett. 15 T 40-41.) p 73

3 October 1781. William LINDSAY and Nancy Shepherd, spinster. Both of St. Thomas' Parish. Sur. William Brockman. p 10

4 September 1773. Willian LINNEY and Ann Bell. Found in Deed Book 17. Both of St. Thomas' Parish. p 203

20 November 1780. Willian LINNEY and Anne Burrus, widow, who gives her own consent. Of St. Thomas' Parish. p 9

17 December 1800. Moses LINTON and Nancy Reed, who writes her own consent. Sur. Joel Durrett. Wit. Reynolds Chapman. p 52

12 November 1793. John LLOYD and Nancy Montague. Sur. Andrew Montague. Wit. James Taylor. p 34

15 October 1809. Thompson LLOYD and Sarah Mowbry. Married by Rev. George Bingham. p 76

7 November 1785. Henry LONG and Lucy Manspoile. Sur. John Long. Wit. Henry Winslow. p 16

10 February 1785. James LONG and Elizabeth Reynolds. Married by Rev. Nathaniel Sanders. p 15

29 December 1796. Richard LONG and Nancy Stevenson. Sur. Joseph Stevenson. Wit. James Taylor, Jr. p 42

20 November 1775. Weir LONG and Anne Sinath. Found in Deed Book 17. Both in St. Thomas' Parish. Notation: by Banns. p 4

3 May 1804. William LONG and Elizabeth Bickers. Sur. Joseph Bickers, who makes oath Elizabeth is over 21; no relationship stated. p 63

25 October 1809. Edmund LONGAN and Sally Edwards. Sur. Joseph Edwards, who makes oath Sally is over 21; no relationship stated. p 76

7 July 1800. Thomas LORRILL and Elizabeth Clee, dau. John Clee, who consents. Sur. William Duke. Wit. William Stanard and Reynolds Chapman. Married by Rev. George Bingham. p 51

13 April 1802. James LOVELL and Elizabeth Harvey. Sur. William Harvey, who makes oath Elizabeth is over 21. Married 15 April by Rev. Hamilton Goss. p 57

2 January 1806. Peter LOWER and Judith Ham. Married by Rev. George Bingham. p 68

24 June 1773. Francis LOWINS and Sarah Davis. Found in Deed Book 17. Both of St. Thomas' Parish. p 203

13 June 1802. Abner LOWRY and Nancy Lowry. Married by Rev. George Bingham. p 57

20 November 1805. Thomas LOWRY and Nancy Dedman, of age, dau. John Dedman, who consents. Sur. Philip Dedman. Married 21 November by Rev. Nathaniel Sanders, Baptist. p 67

18 December 1805. George LOYD and Betsy Bell. Sur. William Pulliam, who makes oath both are over 21. p 67

27 April 1780. Thomas LOYD and Sally Gresham, widow. Both of St. Thomas' Parish. Sur. John Loyd. p 9

25 December 1809. Willis LOYD and Felicia Ayheart. Married by Rev. George Bingham. This name is probably Ahart. p 77

24 July 1801. Elijah LUCAS and Nancy Brockman, dau. William Brockman, who consents and is surety. Wit. Robert Brockman. p 54

24 March 1801. Ezekiel LUCAS and Catharine Ahart. Sur. John Farguson, who makes oath Catharine is 21 years of age. Wit. Reynolds Chapman. Married 29 March by Rev. Hamilton Goss. p 53

24 October 1788. James LUCAS and Nancy Henderson. No surety or witness given. p 22

25 January 1789. Thomas LUCAS and Sally Garnett Snell. Sur. Eastham Snell. Married 9 March by Rev. John Leland. p 23

21 December 1773. William LUCAS and Ann Burbridge. Found in Deed Book 17. Both of St. Thomas' Parish. p 203

31 January 1799. Zachariah LUCAS and Nancy Wood. Married by Rev. Hamilton Goss. p 48

13 November 1798. John MC ALESTER and Cary Turner, dau. Ann Turner, who consents. Sur. James Turner. Wit. Benjamin McAlester and James Taylor. Cary in consent, but Clary in bond. p 47

15 August 1802. John MC CLAMROCK and Jenne Estes, dau. Elisha Estes, who consents. Sur. Caleb Smoot. Wit. George McClamrock. Married 18 August by Rev. George Bingham. p 57

17 December 1795. Robert MC CLARNEY and Sarah Morris. Sur. Archulus Hawkins. p 38

5 November 1801. David MC CLARY and Catey Picker. Married by Rev. George Bingham. p 55

10 March 1788. George MC COY and Elizabeth Nickings, 24 years old, dau. Nathaniel Nickings, who makes affidavit as to her age. Sur. George Marshall. Wit. Merryman Marshall and Robert Jones. Married 11 March by Rev. George Eve. p 21

18 December 1809. Michael MC COYLE and Mary McKinney, dau. William McKinney, who is surety; also makes oath Michael is over 21. p 77

25 September 1793. Derenzey MC DANIEL and Susanna Brooks, dau. John Brooks, who consents. Sur. Joshua Kendle. Wit. George Brooks. p 33

4 December 1799. .Jeremiah MC DANIEL and Rachel Brooks, dau. Jane Brooks, who consents. Sur. Derenzy McDaniel, who makes oath Rachel is 21 years of age. Wit. George Brooks. p 49

11 April 1799. Stacy MC DANIEL and Sally Lamb. Married by Rev. George Bingham. p 48

25 July 1792. Patrick MC DONALD and Elizabeth Miller, dau. Judith Miller, who consents. Sur. John Miller. Wit. James Taylor, Jr. p 30

6 January 1808. William MC FARLANG and Fanny Alsop. Sur. Daniel Cokeley. Wit. John Cokeley. William son of John McFaling, who consents for him. p 72

14 December 1810. John MC FARLING and Frances Dedman, who makes oath she will be 23 on 23 February 1811. Sur. George Herndon. Wit. George Rhodes. p 79

26 December 1796. Hugh MC KINLEY and Anna Rita Finnell. Sur. William Finnell. p 42

7 January 1801. Travis MC KINNEY and Betsy Pollard. Sur. Edmund Pollard. Wit. Reynolds Chapman. p 53

14 March 1796. James MC MULLIAN and Edy Kindoll, dau. Henry and Ruth Kindoll. John McMullan and Edward Briant sign certificate that both are of age. Sur. James Harvey. Wit. Jeremiah Briant and William Lewis Powell. p 39

2 January 1792. Patrick MC MULLAN and Sarah Walker. Sur. Thomas Walker. Consent of John and Theodora (Beasley) McMullan for Patrick. Married 5 January by Rev. George Eve. p 29

28 December 1801. James MACHONEY and Patsey Sleet, dau. James Sleet, Jr. Sur. John Sleet. Wit. Alexander Newman. Married 31 December by Rev. Nathaniel Sanders, Baptist. This name also spelled McHoney in bond. p 56

30 January 1790. Thomas MACON and Sarah Madison, born 17 August 1764, dau. Col. James and Eleanor (Conway) Madison, who were married 13 September 1749. Sur. James Madison (brother). p 25

17 March 1807. Catlett MADISON and Winney J. ROUTT, who writes her own consent. Sur. William Tinsley and Stewart Sanford. Wit. John Allen. Married by Rev. Robert Jones. p 70

9 October 1772. Francis MADISON and Susanna Bell. Found in old fee book by J. W. Browning. Both of St. Thomas' Parish. p 2

30 December 1791. Henry MAGGARD and Betsy Lamb, spinster. Sur. George Argebright. Wit. James Taylor, Jr. Married 1 January 1792 by Rev. George Bingham. p 29

20 November 1802. Samuel MAHANES and Elizabeth Brockman, dau. William Brockman, who consents and is surety. William Lunsford makes oath Samuel is over 21. Married 25 November by Rev. Hamilton Gass. p 58

24 November 1794. Daniel MAHONEY and Fanny Finny. Sur. William Garde. Wit. William Ledders. Married 11 December by Rev. George Eve. p 36

4 April 1804. Elijah MALLORY and Judith Payne. Sur. John Payne, who makes oath Judith is over 21; no relationship stated. p 63

24 December 1781. Henry MALLORY and Lucy Long, widow. Both of St. Thomas' Parish. Sur. John Dear. p 11

18 January 1795. Henry MALLORY and Ann Jones. Married by Rev. George Bingham. p 36

21 December 1801. James MALLORY and Polly Brockman. Sur. John Brockman, Sr., who consents for Polly; no relationship stated. Wit. John Brockman, Jr. and Thomas Brockman. p 55

17 February 1778. John MALLORY and Sarah Sawyer. Found in Deed Book 17. Both of St. Thomas' Parish. p 7

27 February 1804. John MALLORY and Frances Morton. Sur. William Morton. Married by Rev. Nathaniel Sanders. p 62

9 June 1789. Reuben MALLORY and Dorothy Cartee (Carter?). Sur. John Bledose. Wit. James Taylor. p 24

17 October 1798. Robert MALLORY and Nancy Mally. Married by Rev. George Bingham. p 46

16 May 1797. Roger MALLORY and Mary Payne, dau. Thomas Payne, who consents. Sur. Moses Leathers. Wit. Charles Bell. p 43

8 December 1797. William MALLORY and Mary Gibson. John Gibson consents for Mary; no relationship stated. Sur. Uriel Mallory, Jr. Wit. Robert Mallory and James Taylor, Jr. p 44

17 February 1796. Johny MANSPOILE and Sally Wood, dau. Catey Wood, who consents. Sur. Zachariah Lee. Wit. Zachariah Wood. Married 19 February by Rev. Nathaniel Sanders. p 39

9 December 1772. Michael MARKSPILE and Ann Long. Found in Deed Book 17. Both of St. Thomas' Parish. p 203

5 January 1760. Alexander MARR and Sarah Rucker. This license found in an old fee book by J. W. Browning. Both of St. Thomas' Parish. p 1

23 April 1810. Joel MARR and Betsy Miller. Sur. Robert Mallory, who makes oath Betsy is over 21. Married 10 May by Rev. Jacob Watts. p 78

24 December 1810. Thomas MARR and Sally Harvey. Sur. Thomas Harvey, who makes oath Sally is over 21; no relationship stated. Married 3 January 1811 by Rev. George Bingham. p 79

24 March 1806. Peter MARSH and Lucy Walker Jollett, dau. James Jollett, who consents and is surety. Married by Rev. William Douglass, Methodist. p 68

30 September 1787. George MARSHALL and Ann Boswell. Sur. William Loyd. Wit. John Fargerson. p 20

27 December 1804. Henry MARSHALL and Ellen Wood. Married by Rev. George Bingham. p 65

25 January 1810. Henry MARSHALL and Elizabeth Walton. Married by Rev. George Bingham. p 77

26 December 1803. Thomas MARSHALL and Nancy Ancell. Sur. Robert Ancell, who makes oath both are over 21; no relationship stated. Married 27 December by Rev. George Bingham. p 62

6 January 1796. Benjamin MARTIN and Mary Knight, dau. Ephraim Knight, who consents. Sur. Benjamin Jacobs. Wit. Gilson Morris and Matthew Bridges. In consent Ephraim Knight calls his dau. Eliza Ann. p 39

8 July 1793. Brice MARTIN and Rachel Lucas. Sur. William Lucas, Jr. and Isaac Davis, Jr. Wit. James Taylor. Married 7 August by Rev. George Eve. p 33

14 May 1783. George MARTIN and Elizabeth Jones, dau. Thomas Jones, who consents. Sur. John Young. Wit. William Young. Both of St. Thomas' Parish. p 12

30 July 1804. George MARTIN and Fanny Sisson. Sur. Abner Sisson. Wit. George Sisson. Sarah Sisson signs consent for Fanny. Henry Martin signs consent for George. No relationship stated in either case. p 63

3 December 1808. William MARTIN and Patsy Atkins. Sur. Lewis Harris, who makes oath Patsy is over 21. p 74

27 December 1810. William MARTIN and Margaret Snell. Sur. John Snell, who makes oath Margaret is over 21; no relationship stated. Married by Rev. James Goss. p 79

10 August 1797. George MASON and Millicent Sanders, dau. Nathaniel Sanders, who consents. George, brother of Charles Mason, who consents for him. Wit. James Mason and Peter Mason. Sur. Jonathan Preacher. Wit. David Faulconer and John Mason. p 44

25 December 1797. Isam B. MASON and Lucy Sebree, spinster. Martin Johnson consents for Lucy, says she lives with his family and is of age. Sur. William Watts. Married 27 December by Rev. Hamilton Goss. p 45

24 August 1795. James MASON and Nancy Oaks. Sur. Charles Mason. Married 26 August by Rev. Nathaniel Sanders. p 37

27 December 1795. John MASON and Lucy Sebree. Married by Rev. Hamilton Goss. p 38

16 August 1796. John MASON and Elizabeth Faulconer, dau. Thomas Faulconer, who consents. Sur. Samuel Mason. p 40

26 June 1809. Joseph MASON and Anna Tandy, dau. Henry and Ann (Mills) Tandy, who consent. Sur. William Tandy, brother. Wit. Jackson Tandy, brother. Anna b. 6 August 1776. p 75

29 October 1804. Samuel MASON and Lyddia Graves. Sur. Thomas Graves, who makes oath Lyddia is over 21; no relationship stated. p 64

25 December 1797. Jennings MAUPIN and Sally Miller. Sur. Thomas Miller. p 45

24 January 1803. Leonard H. MAURY and Virginia M. Campbell, dau. William Campbell, who consents. Sur. Robert Wilson. p 59

6 February 1792. John MAXWELL and Agatha Henry, who writes her own consent. Sur. Benson Henry. Married by Rev. George Eve. p 29

27 March 1792. Thomas MAXWELL and Dulley Henry, dau. William Henry, who consents. Sur. James Maxwell. Wit. Thomas Herndon. Married 3 April by Rev. George Eve. p 30

12 December 1775. Ambrose MEDLEY and Frankie Burton. Sur. Capt. May Burton, Jr. Wit. Jonathan Taylor and Francis Pendleton. Ambrose of Brumfield Parish; Frankie of St. Thomas' Parish. p 4

13 July 1804. Jacob MEDLEY and Fanny Head, dau. John Head. Sur. Benjamin Burton. Wit. Richard Cave. Married 15 July by Rev. Hamilton Goss. p 63

1 October 1801. William MELBURN and Sarah Taylor. Sur. Charles Taylor. p 54

14 January 1809. William MELONE and Mary Wayland. Henry Wayland signs consent for Mary; no relationship stated. Sur. Matthew Marquess. Wit. Joseph Wayland and Henry Wayland, Jr. Married 22 January by Rev. George Bingham. p 74

20 November 1786. Spencer MENEFEE and Ritta Boston. Sur. Joseph Boston. Wit. James Taylor. p 19

11 September 1800. Charles MERRIWETHER and Ann Minor. Dabney Minor, guardian of Ann, consents for her and is surety. Wit. Reynolds Chapman. p 51

10 October 1804. William MERRYMAN and Elizabeth Stevens. Sur. Merryman Stevens, who makes oath both are over 21. p 64

23 July 1787. John MICHIE and Frances Earley, dau. Theodoshe Earley, who consents. Sur. James Earley. Wit. Leonard Philips and Dorcas Shiflett. p 20

7 June 1808. Christian MILLER and Elizabeth Beazley. Married by Rev. George Bingham. p 73

11 February 1778. Henry MILLER and Margaret Piglen. Found in Deed Book 17. Both of St. Thomas' Parish. Notation: by Banns. p 7

19 January 1796. Jesse MILLER and Ann Stevens, dau. Joseph Stevens, Sr., who consents. Sur. William Stevens. Wit. Merryman Stevens. Married 11 February by Rev. Nathaniel Sanders. p 39

22 December 1794. Thomas MILLER and Sarah Plunkett, dau. Jesse Plunkett, who consents. Sur. William Clark. Wit. Robert Miller. Married 13 January 1795 by Rev. George Eve. p 36

13 July 1802. James C. MILTON and Mary Taylor. Sur. James Taylor, who makes oath Mary is over 21. Married by Rev. Robert Jones. p 57

18 March 1794. Henry MITCHELL and Molly Lucas, dau. William Lucas, Jr., who consents and is surety. Wit. Francis Taylor. Molly in bond, but her father calls her Mary in his consent. p 35

4 February 1805. Thomas MITCHELL and Nancy Rumsey, dau. Thomas Rumsey, who consents. Sur. Marmaduke Branham. Wit. Elijah Rumsey. p 66

21 December 1790. William MITCHELL and Rebecca Grinnels, dau. Sarah Grinnels, who consents. Sur. George Marshall. Wit. Merryman Marshall and Francis Taylor. p 27

31 March 1808. John MOODY and Betsy Stowers, dau. Mark Stowers, who is surety. p 73

13 May 1807. Alexander MOORE and Lucy Ford, dau. William Ford, who consents. Sur. Gowry Waugh. Wit. Francis Ford. Married 15 May by Rev. Nathaniel Sanders, Baptist. p 70

3 October 1770. Bernard MOORE and Catey Price; both of St. Thomas' Parish. This marriage found in an old fee book by J. W. Browning. p 2

9 November 1761. Francis MOORE, Jr. and Lucy Hawkins. This license found in an old fee book by J. W. Browning. Both of St. Thomas' Parish. p 1

29 April 1788. Francis MOORE and Lucy Ward. Married by Rev. George Eve. p 21

19 January 1803. James MOORE and Naney or Nancy James. Joseph James makes oath Nancy is over 21; no relationship stated. Sur. Richard Rhodes. Married by Rev. Nathaniel Sanders, Baptist. p 59

23 January 1798. John MOORE and Elizabeth Smith, spinster. Sur. William Lloyd. Wit. John Pendleton. p 45

1 June 1800. Nathaniel MOORE and Sally Adams, dau. John Adams, who consents. Sur. Richard Richards. Wit. William Williams and William Loyd. p 51

28 June 1793. Robert MOORE and Elizabeth Gaines Spencer, dau. Joseph Spencer, who consents. Sur. Reuben Gaines. Wit. Tanadah Gaines. p 33

16 August 1804. Thomas R. MOORE and Elizabeth Crow. Obadiah Overton, guardian of Elizabeth, consents for her. Sur. John Payne. p 64

10 April 1781. William MOORE and Betsy Johnson Grymes. Both of St. Thomas' Parish. Sur. Ludwell Grymes. p 10

2 June 1803. William MOORE and Susanna Day. Pierce Sanford, guardian of Susanna, consents for her and is surety. Married by Rev. Robert Jones. p 60

2 April 1804. William MOORE and Rebecca Hite Smith, dau. John Smith, who consents and is surety. Married by Rev. Nathaniel Sanders, Baptist. p 63

29 December 1802. Yelly MOORE and Elizabeth Brown, dau. John Brown, who consents. Sur. Cornelius Brown. Wit. Travis Brown. Married 30 December by Rev. Robert Jones. This name is probably Yelverton. p 59

18 February 1776. David MORRIS and Jemima Grunter. Found in Deed Book 17. Both of St. Thomas' Parish. Notation: by Banns. p 6

9 February 1802. Elijah MORRIS and Elizabeth Geer. Married by Rev. George Bingham. p 56

7 April 1795. George MORRIS and Susannah Graves, dau. Richard Graves, who consents. Sur. Joseph Hilman. p 37

15 March 1790. Gilson MORRIS and Molly Knight, dau. Ephraim Knight, who consents. Sur. Thomas Johnson. Wit. Reuben Morris and Johnny Morris. Married 18 March by Rev. John Leland. p 26

21 September 1775. John MORRIS and Linny Brown. Found in Deed Book 17. Both of St. Thomas' Parish. Notation: by Banns. p 4

14 October 1809. John MORRIS, Jr. and Sukey Dollins, dau. William Dollins, who is surety. Married by Rev. James Goss. p 76

28 January 1802. Josiah MORRIS and Suckey Shifflet. Married by Rev. George Bingham. p 56

10 June 1793. Reubin MORRIS and Molly Coleman, dau. James Coleman, who consents. Sur. Jilson Morris. Wit. George Faulkner. p 33

22 December 1806. Reubin MORRIS and Sally Acree, dau. William Acree, who consents and is surety. Married 24 December by Rev. Robert Jones. p 69

1 May 1778. Thomas MORRIS and Peggy Rennolds. Found in Deed Book 17. Both of St. Thomas' Parish. Notation: by Banns. p 8

20 January 1803. Thomas MORRIS and Betsy Acry. Sur. William Acry, who consents for Betsy and makes oath Thomas is over 21; no relationship stated. p 59

3 December 1807. Thomas MORRIS and Sally Wright. Sur. Elisha Wright. Married 14 December by Rev. Robert Jones. p 72

6 February 1802. William Anderson MORRISS and Winneyfret Quisenberry, dau. Aaron Quisenberry. Sur. Roger Slaughter. Wit. Thomas Tutson. p 56

13 April 1791. George MORRISON and Sally Sisson, who writes her own consent. Sur. James Coleman. Wit. James Taylor, Jr. Married 14 April by Rev. Nathaniel Sanders. p 28

31 July 1797. Thomas MORRISON and Nanny Dawson, dau. John Dawson, who consents. Sur. William Dawson. Wit. James Taylor, Jr. p 44

25 September 1797. George MORTON, Jr. and Elizabeth Coleman, dau. Elizabeth Coleman, who consents. Sur. Thomas Coleman. Wit. James Taylor. p 44

24 April 1788. John MORTON, Jr. and Mary Tandy, dau. Henry and Anne (Mills) Tandy. Sur. Henry Tandy. (Henry Tandy b. 6 March 1741, d. 1 July 1809 m. 18 November 1763 Anne Mills b. 18 July 1742, d. 14 December 1810. 15 T 39-40. John Morton, son of John and Elizabeth Hawkins Morton.) p 21

26 October 1803. Robert MORTON and Margaret Curtis. Sur. James Morton, who makes oath Margaret is over 21. p 61

5 January 1775. William MORTON and Milly Taylor. Found in Deed Book 17. Both of St. Thomas' Parish. p 3

8 December 1787. John MOTHERSHED and Suckey Burrus. Sur. Joseph Griffin. Wit. James Taylor. p 25

18 December 1761. Nathaniel MOTHERSHED and Mary Minor. This license found in an old fee book by J. W. Browning. Both of St. Thomas' Parish. p 1

11 August 1781. Nathaniel MOTHERSHED and Ruthey Birt, dau. Moses Birt, who consents. Sur. John Cook. Wit. Henry Cook and Phebe Cook. p 10

23 June 1806. James MOZINGO and Mildred Clemmons, dau. Henry Clemmons. Sur. John Herndon. Wit. John Allen. Married by Rev. Robert Jones. p 68

23 March 1801. Zachariah MURPHY and Lucy Atkins, dau. James Atkins, Jr., who consents. Sur. Nathaniel Middlebrook. Wit. William Webb. p 53

22 July 1776. John MUSICK and Mary Berry. Found in Deed Book 17. Both of St. Thomas' Parish. Notation: by Banns. p 6

31 March 1800. Joseph MUZINGO and Polly Clemens. Sur. Henry Clemens. p 51

15 September 1809. Martin NALLE and Nelly Barbour, who writes her own consent. Sur. J. W. Barbour. p 76

23 August 1785. Charles NEAL and Ann Miller. Sur. Francis Collins. Wit. Jesse Plunkett. Robert Miller consents for Ann; no relationship stated. p 15

22 October 1787. Fielding NEAL and Catherine Beazley, dau. James Beazley, who consents. Sur. Charles Neal. Wit. William Riddell. Married 12 November by Rev. George Eve. p 20

3 August 1782. Miscajah NEAL and Milly Beazley, dau. James Beazley, who consents. Sur. Mace Pickett. Wit. Edmund Beazley and Lewis Riddell. p 11

13 June 1803. William NELSON and Sarah Smith, dau. James Smith. Sur. Elisha Adams. Wit. John Page and George W. Hughes. William, son of James Nelson, who consents for him. p 60

14 March 1803. Alexander NEWMAN and Lucy Sleet, dau. James Sleet, Sr., who consents and is surety. Married by Rev. Nathaniel Sanders, Baptist. p 60

21 July 1801. Andrew NEWMAN and Jinnette Garner, who writes her own consent. Sur. James Fleet, Jr. p 54

3 July 1804. John NEWMAN and Sidnah Quisenberry, dau. George Quisenberry. Sur. Moses Hawkins. Wit. George Quisenberry, Jr. p 63

7 March 1798. Thomas NEWMAN and Lucy Barbour. Sur. John Henshaw. Wit. James Taylor. p 46

22 October 1798. Thomas NEWMAN and Patsey Oliver Morris, dau. George Morris, who consents. Sur. William Morton. Wit. John Bourne. p 47

24 August 1809. William NEWMAN, Jr. and Lucy Faulconer. Sur. Nicholas Faulconer. Married by Rev. Robert Jones. p 76

5 March 1796. Jacob NIPPER and Elizabeth Fleck. Sur. Andrew Fleck. Married 15 March by Rev. George Eve. p 39

23 August 1776. Joseph NOOMES and Rachel Davis. Found in Deed Book 17. Both of St. Thomas' Parish. p 7

1 August 1791. Cuthbert NORMAN and Sophia Jollett. Sur. James Jollett. Married 2 August by Rev. George Eve. p 28

22 September 1806. Mainyard OAKES and Polly Lancaster, dau. John and Susanna Lancaster, who consent. Sur. James Mason. Wit. Benjamin Webb. Married by Rev. Nathaniel Sanders, Baptist. Double Wedding! See William Bennett Webb. p 69

7 April 1807. John OAKS and Joanna Graves, dau. Thomas Graves, who is surety and makes oath Joanna is over 21. Married 14 April by Rev. Nathaniel Sanders, Baptist. p 70

21 December 1792. John OGG, Jr. and Sally Goodall. Sur. John Goodall. p 31

7 June 1793. William OGG and Frankey Lamb, dau. John Lamb, who consents and is surety. Wit. John Lamb, Jr. and Capt. May Burton, Jr. p 33

24 August 1781. James OLIVE and Susannah Minor, spinster. Both of St. Thomas' Parish. Sur. Nathaniel Mothershead. p 10

Achilles OLIVER: see Killis OLIVER

5 September 1792. Caleb OLIVER and Nancy White, dau. Thomas White, who consents. Sur. Richard White. Wit. John White and Shelton White. Married 15 September by Rev. George Eve. p 30

23 Janauary 1797. Killis OLIVER and Winney Riddle, dau. James Riddle, who consents. Sur. Richard White. Wit. James Riddle, Jr. and William Riddle. This name is Achilles Oliver in the bond. p 42

11 December 1783. John ORANT and Peggy Lintor. Sur. Benoni Hansford. Both of St. Thomas' Parish. p 13

5 April 1803. Fielding OSBORNE and Mary Massey, dau. Edmund Massey, who consents and is surety. p 60

27 August 1798. Michael OTT and Catherine Pence. Sur. William Campbell. p 46

27 June 1803. George OVERPACK and Martha Carns. George Walters, guardian of Martha, consents for her and is surety. p 60

2 October 1788. Beverly OVERTON and Elizabeth Connor. Sur. Willis Overton. p 22

15 September 1789. Beverly OVERTON and Patty Richards, dau. William Richards, who consents. Sur. James Jones. Wit. Babin Richards. Married 14 October by Rev. John Leland. p 24

7 February 1797. John OVERTON and Martha Carleton, who writes her own consent. Sur. Willis Overton. Wit. Charles Bell. p 42

15 January 1798. Joshua OVERTON and Frances Farmer, spinster. Sur. Willis Overton. Wit. James Taylor. p 45

1 September 1788. Willis OVERTON and Nancy Bradley. Sur. Reuben Boston. p 22

31 December 1790. John OWENS and Sarah Hambleton, widow. Sur. William Richards. Wit. J. B. Pendleton. p 27

31 March 1795. Sturd OWENS and Caty Harris. Married by Rev. George Bingham. p 37

21 August 1799. John PADGETT and Nancy Beckham. Sur. Benjamin Chisholm. Wit. James Taylor. p 49

23 December 1800. Elijah PAGE and Nelly Sisk, dau. Martin Sisk, who consents. Sur. Jacob Anderson. Wit. Barnett Sisk and Hugh Roberts. Married 25 December by Rev. Hamilton Goss. p 52

3 December 1789. James PAGE and Winny Shiflett. Sur. Lewis Stowers.
Wit. James Taylor. Winny, dau. Elizabeth Shiflett, who consents.
James, son of Elizabeth Page. Bond says both James and Winny of age.
p 25

7 December 1777. John PAGE and Elizabeth Middlebrook. Found in Deed
Book 17. Both of St. Thomas' Parish. Notation: by Banns. p 6

22 December 1783. John PAGE, Jr. and Mary Collings, Jr., dau. Mary
Collings, Sr., who consents. John, son of John Page, Sr. and
Elizabeth Page. Sur. William Alexander. Both of St. Thomas'
Parish. p 13

27 March 1793. William PAGE and Elizabeth Alexander. James and
Elizabeth Alexander consent for Elizabeth; no relationship stated.
Sur. James McMullan. Wit. John McMullan and William B. Knight. p 32

30 January 1800. James PAGGETT and Phillis Beecon. Consent of Elizabeth
Beecon, guardian of Phillis. Both over 21 years of age. Sur.
Benjamin Chisholm. Wit. John Deane and Reynolds Chapman. p 50

15 August 1804. William PAGGETT and Ann Clark, dau. Patrack Clark, who
consents. Sur. Ikey Richards. Wit. Roberson Spalding. William, son
of Ann Paggett, who consents for him. Married 17 August by Rev.
Nathaniel Sanders, Baptist. p 63

17 April 1780. Richard PARKER and Hannah Cave, dau. William Cave, who
consents. Sur. Rowland Thomas, Jr. Wit. Robert Stubblefield and
Charles Thomas. Both of St. Thomas' Parish. p 9

4 August 1774. Winslow PARKER and Mary Thomas. Found in Deed Book 17.
Both of St. Thomas' Parish. p 3

15 January 1810. William PARROTT and Judith Wayland, dau. Joshua
Wayland, who consents. Sur. Henry Wayland. Wit. Willis Wayland
and Rennalls Chapman. Married by Rev. Jacob Watts. p 77

9 December 1800. David PARSONS and Elizabeth Clark. Sur. John Clark.
p 52

3 March 1776. John PATTERSON and Peggy Cudding. Found in Deed Book 17.
Notation: by Banns. Peggy of St. Thomas' Parish; John of Berkely
County. p 6

28 July 1793. Jacob PAUL and Catey Neale, widow. Sur. John Hause.
Wit. James Taylor. Married 15 August by Rev. George Eve. p 33

27 December 1790. Robert PAUL and Rachel Edwards. Sur. Charles Finnell.
Married 28 December by Rev. Nathaniel Sanders. p 27

6 August 1793. John PAYNE and Suckey Lindsay. Sur. Adam Lindsay. Wit. James Taylor. The bride's name was Susanna. p 33

27 July 1801. John PAYNE and Elizabeth Bledsoe (widow). Sur. Ambrose Richards. p 54

1 January 1802. John PAYNE and Mildred Chissam. Sur. Samuel Gamboe. See John Rogers. p 56

8 January 1805. John PAYNE and Elizabeth Mallory. Sur. Elijah Mallory, who makes oath both are over 21; no relationship stated. Married 10 January by Rev. Robert Jones. p 65

24 July 1809. Robert PAYNE and Ann Collins. Sur. Lewis D. Collins, who makes oath Ann is over 21; no relationship stated. p 75

25 March 1795. William PAYNE and Nancy Foster. Sur. Joseph Canterberry. Wit. Jacob Holsapple and Abraham Housworth. William, son of Richard Payne, who consents. p 37

17 October 1801. Edmund PEACHER and Lucy Hilman, dau. Joseph Hilman, who consents. Sur. Uriel Hilman. Wit. William Hilman. Married 20 October by Rev. Nathaniel Sanders, Baptist. p 54

27 December 1791. Reuben PEACHER and Sarah Johnson, dau. Nancy Johnson, who consents. Sur. James Jones. Wit. Thomas Johnson. Married 29 December by Rev. Nathaniel Sanders. p 29

10 September 1789. John PEARSON and Betsy Goodridge, "21 years of age"; writes her own consent. Sur. Killis Oliver. Wit. Priscilla Franklin. p 24

24 February 1778. Jacob PECK and Polly Coursey. Found in Deed Book 17. Polly of St. Thomas' Parish. Jacob of Staunton. p 7

13 April 1795. John PENCE and Elizabeth Lucas, who writes her own consent. Sur. Zacharish Lucas. Wit. Chariah Lucas and Hobton Goodrige. John Pence of age. p 37

2 June 1796. Benjamin PENDLETON and Elizabeth Quisenberry, dau. William Quisenberry, who consents. Sur. James Taylor. p 40

8 November 1785. John PENDLETON and Elizabeth Taylor. Sur. James Taylor. p 16

22 December 1806. John PENDLETON and Fanny Thompson, who writes her own consent. Sur. Jackson Tandy, who makes oath Fanny is over 21. Wit. Henry Tandy, Sr. p 69

3 November 1788. Rice PENDLETON and Elizabeth Quisenberry, dau. John Quisenberry, who consents. Sur. George Quisenberry. p 22

31 January 1797. Robert PENDLETON and Elizabeth Burrus. Sur. Edmund Burrus. p 42

2 January 1798. Charles PERCEY and Elizabeth Lower, dau. Michael Lower, who consents. Sur. Jacob Lower. Wit. Charles Bell. p 45

18 July 1797. Abraham PERRY and Polly Wharton, dau. George Wharton, who consents. Sur. Moses Bledsoe. Wit. John Bledsoe and Benjamin Bledsoe. p 43

9 January 1797. Elijah PERRY and Ann Webb, dau. Richard Crittenden Webb, who consents. Sur. James Mason. Wit. James Taylor, Jr. Elijah, son of James Perry, who consents. p 42

28 February 1791. James PERRY and Nancy Tandy. Sur. Roger Tandy (brother). Wit. James Taylor. (Nancy b. 6 October 1768, dau. Henry and Ann Mills Tandy, who m. 18 November 1763. His will Orange County Will Book 4 p 331. 14 T 120.) p 27

22 February 1773. Lewis PERRY and Mary Burrows. Found in Deed Book 17. Both of St. Thomas' Parish. p 203

23 March 1786. Moses PERRY and Susa Brockman. Sur. Samuel Brockman. p 18

27 October 1790. Peter PERRY and Lucy Faulconer. Sur. David Faulconer. Married 4 November by Rev. Nathaniel Sanders. p 26

2 September 1773. George PETTY and Elizabeth McNeal. Found in Deed Book 17. Both of St. Thomas' Parish. p 203

26 March 1804. Zachary PETTY and Polly Kendel, dau. John Kendel. Sur. James Sleet, Jr. Wit. Joshua Kendel. p 63

14 July 1806. Conyers PHILIPS and Elizabeth Farneyhough (or Fearney), dau. Thomas Fearney, who consents. Sur. John Fearney. Wit. William Lucas. Married by Rev. Jacob Watts. p 68

2 March 1778. David PHILIPS and Mary Davis. Found in Deed Book 17. Both of St. Thomas' Parish. p 8

16 November 1791. Thomas PHILLIPS and Milly Davis, dau. Jonathan and Milly Davis, who consent. Sur. David Philips. Wit. James Taylor. H. Thomas Philips signs consent for Thomas; no relationship stated. p 29

18 November 1799. Thomas PHIPS and Polly Montague. Sur. John Montague. p 49

26 December 1803. William PIPER and Elizabeth White. Sur. Willis White, who makes oath Elizabeth is over 21; no relationship stated. Married 29 December by Rev. Jacob Watts. p 62

3 November 1788. Jonathan PITCHER and Betsy Mason. Sur. Charles Mason. p 22

19 November 1803. William PITCHER and Fanny Coleman, dau. James Coleman, who consents and is surety. Wit. James and Sally Coleman. p 61

26 December 1794. Edmund POLLARD and Sally Herndon, spinster. Writes her own consent. Sur. Benjamin Wright. p 36

11 January 1803. Benjamin PORTER and Patsy Newman. Sur. William Newman, who makes oath Patsy is over 21; no relationship stated. Married by Rev. Robert Jones. p 59

4 December 1797. Camp PORTER and Fanny Alcock. John Alcock consents for Fanny; no relationship stated. Sur. John Bourne. p 44

11 November 1782. Charles PORTER, Jr. and Betsy Proctor, dau. George Proctor, who consents. Sur. Benoni Hansford. Both of St. Thomas' Parish. p 11

24 December 1793. John PORTER and Catherine Carter, who writes her own consent. Sur. Pierce Sanford. Wit. Camp Porter. p 34

22 August 1796. William PORTER and Polly McCauley Duncanson. Sur. Charles Urquart. Wit. James Taylor. p 40

24 January 1786. John PULTER and Patsy Ransdell. Sur. Sanford Ransdell. Wit. Francis Taylor. Married 25 January by Rev. John Price. p 18

8 September 1783. Ambrose POWELL and Sally Britt, dau. Mary Britt, who consents. Sur. James Bush. Wit. Mace Pickett, Jr. and Matthew Paulleck. Ambrose, son of Thomas Powell, who consents. Both of St. Thomas Parish. p 13

20 December 1792. Benjamin POWELL and Esther Pickett, dau. Mace Pickett, who consents. Sur. Thomas Walker. Wit. William Cave and Edmund Taylor. Married 24 December by Rev. George Eve. p 31

6 March 1801. Felden POWELL and Susannah Ballard. Sur. Elijah Powell. Wit. Reynolds Chapman. Married 8 March by Rev. Hamilton Goss. The groom signed Fealden Powell. p 53

1 February 1803. John West POWELL and Eliza F. P. Bell, dau. John Bell, who consents. Sur. St. Clair Kirtley. Wit. John Williams. John West Powell of Madison County. p 59

1 January 1793. Lewis Gorden POWELL and Sally Powell, dau. Benjamin Powell, who consents. Sur. Thomas Walker. Wit. William Lewis Powell. Honorias Powell and James Taylor. p 31

23 December 1793. Ptolomey POWELL and Sidney Lavit, widow. Sur. Robert Daniel. p 34

20 December 1800. Reuben POWELL and Elizabeth Ballard, dau. Mourman and Martha Ballard, who consent. Sur. Ezekiah Crafford. Wit. Reynolds Chapman. Married 21 December by Rev. Hamilton Goss. p 52

19 September 1796. William Lewis POWELL and Mary McMullan. John McMullan consents for Mary and is surety; no relationship stated. Wit. Charles Bell. Married 22 September by Rev. George Bingham. p 41

30 March 1805. Thomas PRICE and Elizabeth Dohoney, dau. Hanner Dohoney, who consents. Sur. John Ballard. Married 2 April by Rev. George Bingham. p 66

7 April 1798. Benjamin PRITCHETT and Polly Herndon, who writes her own consent. Sur. William H. Stanard. Wit. Thomas Bartlett. (This was Mary Herndon b. ca. 1773 dau. John and Mary (Lewis) Herndon. The groom was Benjamin Alexander Pritchett.) p 46

29 June 1807. George PROCTOR, Jr. and Fanny Grady, dau. William Grady, Sr., who consents. Sur. John Grady. Wit. Thomas Grady. Married 1 July by Rev. Nathaniel Sanders, Baptist. p 71

30 March 1783. Hezekiah PROCTOR and Nancy Young, dau. John Young, who consents. Sur. John Turnley. Wit. Thomas Jones. Both of St. Thomas' Parish. p 12

22 August 1776. Uriah PROCTOR and Martha Singleton. Found in Deed Book 17. Both of St. Thomas' Parish. Notation: by Banns. p 7

8 May 1777. William PROCTOR and Elizabeth Hiatt. Found in Deed Book 17. Both of St. Thomas' Parish. Notation: by Banns. p 5

3 September 1779. William QUARLES and Frances Vivion. Both of St. Thomas' Parish. Sur. Nathaniel Mills. Wit. Henry Tandy. Frances, dau. John Vivion, who consents. p 8

21 March 1809. George QUICK and Mildred Rains, dau. Reubin Rains, who consents. Sur. Richard Lamb. Wit. Charles Parrott. Married 22 March by Rev. George Bingham. p 75

2 December 1809. Garland QUINN and Dealen Smith. Hannah Hensley consents for Dealen; no relationship stated. Sur. Cypress Hensley. Married 24 December by Rev. Jacob Watts. p 7

27 March 1783. Richard QUINN and Ann Wood. Sur. William Glass. Married 2 April by Rev. J. Price. p 12

17 October 1805. Aaron QUISENBERRY and Henrietta Reynolds, dau. William Reynolds, who consents. Sur. George Quisenberry. Wit. George Quisenberry, Jr. p 67

22 May 1783. George QUISENBERRY and Jane Daniel. Sur. Vivion Daniel. Both of St. Thomas' Parish. p 12

22 June 1802. George QUISENBERRY and Margaret Reynolds, dau. William Reynolds, who consents. Sur. John Young. Wit. Robert Young. p 57

2 December 1776. James QUISENBERRY and Jane Burrows. Found in Deed Book 17. Both of St. Thomas' Parish. Notation: by Banns. (Jane b. 5 July 1759, dau. Thomas Burruss and his wife Frances Tandy. 14 T 119.) p 7

14 August 1805. Moses QUISENBERRY and Milly Durrett, dau. Joel Durrett, who consents and is surety. Wit. J. N. Assam and James Quisenberry. Moses of Louisa County; his guardian, Henry Quisenberry, consents for him. p 66

19 March 1799. Merry RAINES and Anne Floyd. Sur. Samuel Floyd. Married 21 March by Rev. Hamilton Goss. p 48

22 May 1783. Richard RAINS and Theodosia Eastridge. Married by Rev. George Eve, Baptist. p 12

17 April 1807. Richard RAWLINGS and Lucy Herndon. John Herndon, guardian of Lucy, consents for her and is surety. Wit. John Allen. Married 26 April by Rev. Robert Jones. p 70

22 October 1802. William READ and Dysa Rumsey. Sur. Henry Teel, who makes oath Dysa is over 21. p 58

26 December 1796. Isaac READER and Susannah Mackelaney. John Wooffrey, step-father of Susannah, consents for her. Sur. William Hutchinson. Wit. Benjamin Reader. p 41

23 February 1773. Benjamin RENNOLDS and Elizbeth Jennings. Found in Deed Book 17. Both of St. Thomas' Parish. p 203

13 August 1784. Aaron REYNOLDS and Caty Chambers, over 21, who writes her own consent. Sur. James Adams. p 14

23 January 1774. John REYNOLDS and Anna Darnell. Found in Deed Book 17. Notation: by Banns. Both of St. Thomas' Parish. p 2

10 February 1774. Joseph REYNOLDS and Susanna Wright. Found in Deed Book 17. Notation: by Banns. Both of St. Thomas' Parish. p 2

24 August 1778. Richard REYNOLDS and Ann Roach, widow. Found in Deed
Book 17. Both of St. Thomas' Parish. Sur. Thomas Farish. p 8

24 December 1800. Richard REYNOLDS and Lucy Finnell, dau. Simon Finnell,
who consents. Sur. William Dawson. Wit. John Dawson. Lucy is of
age. p 52

1 March 1805. Washington REYNOLDS and Catherine Dent Swann. Sur.
William W. Reynolds. (Catherine, dau. of Samuel Hatch Swann, son
of Samuel Swann of St. Mary's County, Maryland. Washington, son of
Joseph and Susannah (Wright) Reynolds and grandson of Joseph and
Elizabeth (Herndon) Reynolds.) p 66

22 May 1777. William REYNOLDS and Nancy Nixon. Found in Deed Book 17.
Both in St. Thomas' Parish. Notation: by Banns. p 5

27 July 1797. William REYNOLDS and Peggy Rumsey, of age, dau. Thomas
Rumsey, who consents. Sur. Reuben Scott. Wit. James Taylor. p 44

24 January 1803. William REYNOLDS and Jane Quisenberry, dau. George
Quisenberry, who consents and is surety. (William, son of Joseph
and Susanna (Wright) Reynolds and grandson of Joseph and Elizabeth
(Herndon) Reynolds.) p 59

27 November 1809. William REYNOLDS, Jr. and Joice Quisenberry, dau.
Sally Quisenberry, who consents. Sur. Robert Young. Wit. Aaron
Quisenberry and Robert Adams. (William, Jr. son of William Reynolds,
Sr. and his wife Nancy Nixon, grandson of Joseph and Elizabeth
(Herndon) Reynolds.) p 76

28 March 1791. George RHODES and Nancy Wright, dau. B. Bennett, who
consents. Sur. William Wright. Married 1 April by Rev. Nathaniel
Sanders. p 28

10 May 1793. John RHODES and Tabitha Pearson, dau. Robert Pearson, who
consents. Sur. Joseph Burton. Wit. John Eddins. p 32

9 February 1793. Richard RHODES and Lucy Wright. Sur. George Bledsoe
Wright. Wit. James Taylor. p 31

27 May 1782. Robert RHODES and Lesza Delaney, spinster. Sur. Andrew
Shepherd. Robert Rhodes of Albemarle County. p 11

18 December 1797. Ike RICHARDS and Elizabeth Robinson, dau. John
Robinson, who consents. Sur. William Robinson. Wit. Anthony Tinder
and William Richards. Double Wedding: see Anthony Tinder. p 44

3 April 1776. John RICHARDS and Milly Watts. Found in Deed Book 17.
Both of St. Thomas' Parish. Notation: by Banns. p 6

3 February 1778. Philemon RICHARDS and Susanna Woods. Found in Deed Book 17. Both of St. Thomas' Parish. Notation: by Banns. p 7

13 February 1795. Fielding RIDDLE and Milly Waits. Sur. William Lewis Powell. Wit. James Taylor, Jr. Married 17 February by Rev. George Eve. p 36

27 November 1788. James RIDDELL and Theodosia Rhodes. Sur. Charles Neale. Married by Rev. George Eve. p 23

24 September 1804. John RIDDLE and Elizabeth Seal. Sur. John M. Ballard, who makes oath both are over 21. p 64

11 November 1809. Valentine RIDDLE and Betsy Goodall, dau. James Goodall, Sr, who consents. Sur. James Goodall, Jr. and Tavener Riddle. Married by Rev. George Bingham. p 76

25 December 1783. William RIDDELL and Joyce Riddell. Lewis Riddle, uncle of Joyce, consents for her. Sur. John Goodall. Both in St. Thomas' Parish. p 13

24 January 1787. Edward RIGHT and Frankey Powell, dau. John Powell, who consents. Sur. Richard Playle. p 19

28 February 1785. James RIGHT and Sarah Rawson, who writes her own consent. Sur. Luke Jennings. Married 3 March by Rev. Nathaniel Sanders. p 15

25 May 1801. Peter RIPPETO and Martha Taylor, dau. William Taylor, who consents. Sur. Ellis Hambleton. Wit. William Hambleton and Edward Hambleton. p 53

12 April 1797. William RIPPETO and Betsey Strow. Her father consents in German. Sur. William Lucas, Jr. Wit. John Shislor, James Taylor and Charles Bell. p 43

25 July 1792. John RIXEY and Betsy Sutherland. Sur. Joseph Sutherland. Wit. James Taylor, Jr. p 30

22 December 1788. James ROACH and Betsy Lindsay. Sur. Caleb Lindsay. p 23

24 December 1775. Thomas ROBBINS and Mary Foster. Found in Deed Book 17. Both of St. Thomas' Parish. Notation: by Banns. p 5

6 December 1792. George ROBERTS and Luvina Tippett, dau. Samuel Tippett, who consents. Sur. James Powell. Wit. John Roberts. Married 27 December by Rev. George Eve. p 31

2 January 1799. Hugh ROBERTS and Elizabeth Silk. Married by Rev. Hamilton Goss. p 48

30 January 1794. John ROBERTS and Nancy White. Sur. John White. Married by Rev. George Eve. p 34

8 January 1796. John ROBERTS and Agnes Knight, dau. Matthew Knight, who consents. Sur. Samuel Ham. Wit. James Taylor, Jr. p 39

27 December 1790. Thomas ROBERTS and Frances Henry, dau. William Henry, who consents. This is consent only. p 27

28 December 1801. Joseph ROBERTSON and Philadelphia Snell. Sur. Robert Snell, who makes oath Philadelphia is over 21. p 56

5 March 1787. John ROBERTSON and Frances Porter. Sur. Joseph Thomas, Jr. p 19

23 September 1799. Richard ROBERTSON and Elizabeth Collins, spinster. Sur. Edward Collins. p 49

28 February 1788. Francis ROBINSON and Mary Terrell, dau. William Terrell. Sur. John Morton. Wit. James Nelson and John Davis. p 21

16 January 1760. James ROBINSON and Judy Embry. This license found in an old fee book by J. W. Browning. Both of St. Thomas' Parish. p 1

24 November 1757. John ROBINSON and Lucy Smith. This license found in an old fee book by J. W. Browning. Both of St. Thomas' Parish. p 1

20 December 1799. Michael ROBINSON and Polly Williams. Sur. William Arnett. Wit. Reynolds Chapman, who makes oath Polly is over 21 years of age. p 50

24 February 1806. Moses ROBINSON and Fanny Jones, dau. Richard Jones, who consents. Sur. John Campbell. Wit. Reubin Jones. Married 27 February by Rev. James Garnett. p 68

25 April 1777. Thomas ROBINSON and Lucy Robinson. Found in Deed Book 17. Both of St. Thomas' Parish. p 5

27 January 1757. William ROBINSON and Agnes Smith. This license found in an old fee book by J. W. Browning. Both of St. Thomas' Parish. p 1

24 March 1788. William ROBINSON and Franky Adams. James Adams consents for Franky and is surety; no relationship stated. p 21

26 November 1794. William ROBINSON and Margaret Collins, dau. Richard Collins, who consents. Sur. James Herndon. Wit. Betsy Morris and James Taylor, Jr. p 36

24 December 1798. Hugh ROEBUCK and Elizabeth Sisk. Sur. Thomas Roberts. p 47

13 September 1808. Benjamin ROGERS and Mary Lane. Married by Rev. George Bingham. p 73

24 December 1809. Jermenius ROGERS and Elizabeth Farguson. Married by Rev. George Bingham. p 77

31 October 1773. John ROGERS and Barbara Estis. Found in Deed Book 17. Barbara of St. Thomas' Parish; John of Frederickville Parish. p 203

27 December 1798. John ROGERS and Elizabeth Knight. Married by Rev. George Bingham. p 47

30 December 1801. John ROGERS and Mildred Chissom, dau. John Chissom, who consents. Wit. Benjamin Spiar and Samuel Gamboe. This is consent only. See John Payne. p 56

28 February 1803. John ROGERS, Jr. and Lucy Darnel, dau. Mary Darnel, who consents. Sur. James Hunt, who makes oath John Rogers is over 21. p 60

28 June 1808. Joseph ROGERS and Burlinda Newman. Married by Rev. Robert Jones. p 73

12 January 1807. Kelles ROGERS and Mary Ham, dau. Samuel and Eliza Hamm, who consent. Sur. Joseph Ham. Wit. Eliza Ham. Married 15 January by Rev. George Bingham. p 70

10 December 1796. Samuel ROGERS and Sally Davis. Married by Rev. George Bingham. p 41

22 October 1810. Thomas ROGERS and Penelope Chancellor. Thomas Rogers, guardian of Penelope, consents for her. Sur. John Chancellor. Married by Rev. Jeremiah Chandler. p 79

26 January 1801. Robert H. ROSE and Frances F. Madison. Sur. Reynolds Chapman. (Frances born 4 October 1774, dau. Col. James and Eleanor (Conway) Madison, who were married 13 September 1749. She was their 10th and youngest child.) p 53

22 January 1798. Archelaus ROSSON and Haney Ritter Warren, dau. Elizabeth Warren, who consents. Sur. Reuben Moore. Wit. William Perry and James Taylor. p 45

30 October 1793. George ROTHROCK and Elizabeth Pollock, dau. William Pollock, Sr., who consents. Sur. William Cooper. Wit. James Taylor. p 34

23 May 1809. Belfield RUCKER and Nancy White, of age, dau. Richard and Nancy White, who consent. Sur. William Rucker. Wit. John Lucas and John Taylor. Belfield, son of Joel Rucker. Married 28 May by Rev. Ambrose Brockman of Albemarle County. p 75

6 May 1789. Elliot RUCKER and Nancy Smith. Sur. Samuel Smith. Wit. James Taylor. p 24

16 January 1809. Ellzy RUCKER and Mary P. Burton, dau. Joseph Burton, who consents. Sur. James White. Married 19 January by Rev. Jacob Watts. p 74

25 June 1775. Ephraim RUCKER and Elizabeth Randall. Found in Deed Book 17. Both of St. Thomas' Parish. Notation: by Banns. p 4

15 December 1786. Joel RUCKER and Nancy Oliver, dau. Tabitha Oliver, who consents. Sur. Joseph Burton. Wit. Richard White. Married 20 December by Rev. George Eve. p 19

27 April 1780. John RUCKER and Betty Tinsley, spinster. Sur. James Rucker. Wit. Joseph Rucker, Edmund Brown, George Alexander and Garard Morton. John Tinsley consents for Betty; no relationship stated. Both of St. Thomas' Parish. p 9

3 January 1773. Peter RUCKER and Jemimah Crawford. Found in Deed Book 17. Both of St. Thomas' Parish. p 203

22 December 1794. William RUCKER and Catey Taliaferro Thornton, dau. George Thornton, who consents. Sur. George M. Head. Wit. Capt. May Burton, Jr. and Baldwin Buckner. Married 25 December by Rev. George Eve. p 36

29 September 1787. Wisdom RUCKER and Rosanna Burrus, dau. Mary Burrus, who consents. Sur. Vincent Vass. Wit. Thomas Rucker, Jr. p 20

30 July 1805. Elijah RUMSEY and Sally Hughs, dau. Francis Hughs, who consents. Sur. Marmaduke Branham. Wit. Reubin Faulconer. p 66

7 April 1790. James RUMSEY and Mary Deering. Robert Deering consents for Mary; no relationship stated. Sur. Reuben Deering. p 26

15 March 1777. Thomas RUMSEY and Patty Cope. Found in Deed Book 17. Both in St. Thomas' Parish. Notation: by Banns. p 5

28 July 1807. Walker RUMSEY and Polly Camike, who was 21 on 15 May last. Writes her own consent. Sur. Spencer Kelly. p 71

12 May 1790. William RUMSEY and Peggy Barrett. Sur. William Leathers. Wit. John Pendleton. Married 20 May by Rev. John Leland. p 26

11 August 1775. Nehemiah RUSSELL and Sally Collins. Found in Deed Book 17. Both of St. Thomas' Parish. Notation: by Banns. p 4

21 March 1789. William RUSSELL and Mary Merry. Sur. Thomas Herndon. Wit. James Taylor. p 24

6 June 1804. Elijah SAMPSON and Annay Rodgers, dau. John Rodgers. Sur. Alexander Rodgers. Wit. William Gear and Cambay (?) Rodgers. p 63

27 June 1800. James SAMPSON and Anney James. Married by Rev. George Bingham. p 51

23 July 1791. Thomas SAMPSON and Winny Powell. Sur. Thomas Walker. Wit. Frances Taylor. Married 28 July by Rev. George Eve. p 28

8 January 1809. William SAMPSON and Sally Jollet. Married by Rev. George Bingham. p 74

25 September 1810. William SAMPSON, Jr. and Sally Sampson, dau. William Sampson, Sr., who consents. Sur. Cornelius Beazley. Wit. Joseph B. Proctor and William Anderson. p 78

22 September 1785. John SAMS and Mary Bledsoe, dau. Aaron Bledsoe, who consents. Sur. George Terrill. Wit. Mille Weatherall. p 16

18 December 1804. Benjamin SANDERS and Nancy Jones, dau. Francis Jones, who consents. Sur. John Gaines. Wit. John Sanders, Robert Sanders and Richard Faulconer. Rev. Nathaniel Sanders consents for Benjamin; no relationship stated. p 65

17 January 1810. Hamlet SANFORD and Phebe Biggers, dau. Macon Biggers. Sur. Thornton Tucker. Wit. Betsy Tucker. Married by Rev. Robert Jones. p 77

30 June 1788. John SANFORD and Betsy Ransdell, dau. John Ransdell, Sr., who consents. Sur. Ambrose Clark. Wit. Wharton Ransdell and John Ransdell, Jr. p 22

3 January 1804. Muse SANFORD and Betty Scott, dau. George Scott. Sur. John Lucas. Wit. John Lucas, Jr. Married 4 January by Rev. Jacob Watts. p 62

2 March 1789. Reuben SANFORD and Frances Webb, dau. William Crittenden Webb and Jane Vivian Webb, who consent. Sur. John Snell. Married 5 March by Rev. George Eve. p 24

24 December 1800. Reuben SANFORD and Nancy Wallace, dau. James Wallace, Sr., who consents. Sur. Thomas Arnold. Wit. James Sanford and Reynolds Chapman. p 52

28 April 1792. Robert SANFORD and Hannah Grymes. Sur. James Taylor. Wit. William Burton and Fortunatus Winkay. (?) Ludwell Grymes consents for Hannah; no relationship stated. p 30

27 October 1803. Stewart SANFORD and Anna Arnold, dau. Benjamin and Sally Arnold, who consent. Sur. Willis Arnold. Wit. Richard Harrod. Steward in the register, but bond signed Stewart. p 61

21 February 1775. William SAWYER and Elizbeth Wright. Found in Deed Book 17. Both of St. Thomas' Parish. Notation: by Banns. p 3

8 March 1810. Joseph H. SCHOOLER and Dolly Quisenberry. Sur. Henry Quisenberry, who makes oath Dolly is over 21; no relationship stated. Married 13 March by Rev. Jeremiah Chandler. p 77

29 December 1787. George SCOTT and Nancy Wood. Sur. William Scott. p 21

15 October 1807. George SCOTT and Nancy Abell. Sur. George Smith, who makes oath Nancy is over 21. p 71

13 February 1781. Reuben SCOTT and Margaret Cope, spinster. Both of St. Thomas' Parish. Sur. Lewis Cook. p 10

10 February 1791. William SCOTT and Nelly Shadrack. Sur. John Shadrick. Wit. James Taylor. Married by Rev. Nathaniel Sanders. p 27

17 March 1791. John SEBREE and Sally Johnson. Sur. William Tomlinson. Wit. George Tomlinson. John, son of Richard Sebree, who consents. p 27

31 May 1774. William SEBREE and Hannah Kavenner. Found in Deed Book 17. Notation: by Banns. Both of St. Thomas' Parish. p 3

27 June 1775. William SEBREE and Mary Strother. Found in Deed Book 17. Both of St. Thomas' Parish. Notation: by Banns. p 4

21 December 1787. Samuel SELF and Frances Shiflett, dau. Elizabeth Shiflett, who consents. Sur. Mace Pickett. Wit. Lewis Stowers. Married 26 December by Rev. George Eve. p 20

15 July 1796. Christopher SERVERS and Sarah Pierce. Sur. Adam Manspoile. Wit. James Taylor. Married 18 July by Rev. Nathaniel Sanders. p 40

23 July 1794. Edmund SHACKLEFORD and Sally Holliday, who gives her own consent. Sur. James Early. Wit. James Taylor, Jr. p 35

7 January 1789. John SHADRACH and Elizabeth Sanders, spinster. Sur. James Tinder. Wit. John Pendleton. Married by Rev. John Leland. p 23

21 July 1795. Thomas SHADRICH and Sarah Sanders, dau. Nathaniel Sanders, who consents. Sur. John Wharton. Wit. Richard Forkner (Faulconer?) and David Forkner (Faulconer?). p 37

23 September 1805. Jesse SHARMAN and Sally Breeding. Sur. Berryman Breeding, who makes oath both are over 21. Married by Rev. George Bingham. p 67

11 July 1783. Elisha SHARMARARD and Elisa Powell. Married by Rev. George Eve, Baptist. p 12

25 May 1788. John SHELLER and Ann Cox. Sur. Thomas Cox. p 21

2 February 1808. Thomas SHELTON and Clary Beadles, dau. John Beadles, who consents. Sur. Robert M. Beadles. p 72

7 May 1793. Alexander SHEPHERD and Mary Burnley, dau. Zachary Burnley, who consents. Sur. James Burnley. Wit. Francis Taylor. p 32

25 November 1793. George SHEPHERD and Ann Porter, who writes her own consent. Sur. Camp Porter. Wit. John Porter. p 34

8 November 1810. James SHEPHERD and Susan Verdier. William Shepherd, guardian of James, is surety. p 79

30 July 1796. Robert SHER and Jane Addison, 21 years of age. Sur. Archelaus Rosen. Married 31 July by Rev. Nathaniel Sanders. p 40

27 October 1796. John SHIFFLET and Susanna Davis. Married by Rev. George Bingham. p 41

15 September 1798. John SHIFFLET and Ann Hicks. Married by Rev. George Bingham. p 47

29 December 1798. John SHIFFLET and Rhoda Shifflet. No bondsman or witness. p 48

19 January 1809. Overton SHIFFLET and Sally Herring, dau. William R. Herring. Wit. Charles Parrott and James Herring. p 74

1 August 1797. Powell SHIFFLET and Catherine McMullan, dau. John McMullan, who consents. This is consent only. p 44

18 January 1795. Stephen SHIFFLET and Rachel Hicks. Married by Rev. George Bingham. p 36

22 June 1795. Pickett SHIFLETT and Lucretia Powell. Sur. Francis Powell. Wit. James Taylor, Jr. Married 25 June by Rev. George Eve. p 37

27 April 1809. Lewis SHISLER and Sally Clark, dau. Joseph Clark, who is surety. p 75

4 December 1757. John SHROPSHIRE and Mary Porter. This license found in an old fee book by J. W. Browning. Both of St. Thomas' Parish. p 1

14 October 1785. Stephen SILVEY and Frankey Dear. Sur. John Dear. p 16

13 October 1801. William SILVEY and Mary Adkisson, dau. John Adkisson, who consents. Sur. Barnett Adkisson. Wit. William Adkisson and Sarah Adkisson. Married 15 October by Rev. Hamilton Goss. p 54

13 October 1796. Elijah SIMMANDS and Lucy Sandage. Married by Rev. George Bingham. p 41

25 February 1797. Ephraim SIMMANDS and Sarah Hanes. Married by Rev. George Bingham. p 43

14 March 1810. Aaron SIMPSON and Mary Mullican. Sur. John Richards, who makes oath Mary is over 21. Married by Rev. Jeremiah Chandler. p 78

3 May 1800. Daniel SIMPSON and Elizabeth Jones. Sur. James Jones. Wit. Reynolds Chapman. p 51

8 December 1798. William SIMPSON and Ann Thompson, dau. George Thompson, who consents. Sur. John Johnson. Wit. Joel Thompson and Charles Bell.

5 January 1809. Isaac SIMS and Nancy Catterton. Married by Rev. George Bingham. p 74

15 January 1789. Jeremiah SIMS and Margaret Taylor. Married by Rev. George Eve. p 23

10 November 1801. John SIMS and Betty Beazley, widow. Sur. Thomas Cave. Wit. Benjamin Henry. John, son of William Sims, who consents. Married 12 November by Rev. George Bingham. p 55

18 August 1796. Nathaniel SIMS and Susanna Johnson. Married by Rev. George Bingham. p 40

22 December 1787. William SIMS, Jr. and Nancy Watts. John Douglass, father-in-law, (step-father) of Nancy consents for her. Sur. John Pendleton. Wit. Nancy Barydel and Mildred Jones. William, son of William Sims, Sr. p 20

13 February 1796. William SIMS and Fanny Walker, dau. Elizabeth Walker, who consents. Sur. Elijah Page. Wit. Jerry Sims. Married 24 February by Rev. George Eve. p 39

15 February 1790.   John SIMSON and Polly Stev. Dawson, spinster, grand-dau. Thomas Weltch.   Sur. John Dawson.   Wit. John Faulconer and John Chissam.   Married 18 February by Rev. John Leland.   p 25

- - 1771-74. -   SISSON and Millie Braham.   This marriage found on a flyleaf of a memorandum book in Orange County Court House by J. W. Browning.   p 17

31 October 1773.   James SLEET and Ann Foord.   Found in Deed Book 17. Both of St. Thomas' Parish.   p 203

27 October 1804.   James SLEET, Jr. and Rebecca Petty, dau. George Petty, who consents.   Sur. Andrew Newman.   Wit. Abner Petty.   p 64

22 January 1800.   John SLEET and Frances Wright.   William Wright consents for Frances; no relationship stated.   Sur. Bledsoe Wright.   p 50

22 December 1802.   Reuben SLEET and Frances Mallory, dau. Henry Mallory, who consents.   Sur. William Long.   Wit. Richard Chandler.   p 58

21 November 1799.   Weedon SLEET and Patsy Petty, dau. George Petty, who consents.   Sur. John Petty.   Wit. Abner Petty.   Married by Rev. Nathaniel Sanders.   p 49

1 June 1776.   William SMILEY and Esten Norwell.   Found in Deed Book 17. Both in St. Thomas' Parish.   Notation: by Banns.   p 6

25 October 1781.   Absalom SMITH and Jestin Chandler, dau. Joseph Chandler, who consents.   Sur. Edmund Dear.   Wit. John Dear and Robert Chandler.   This name may be Justine.   Both of St. Thomas' Parish. p 10

16 June 1804.   Absalom SMITH and Martha McNiel.   Sur. William Terrill, Jr., who makes oath Martha is over 21.   p 63

19 June 1783.   Charles SMITH and Jane Morton, dau. Elijah Morton, who consents.   Sur. Joseph Morton.   Wit. George Morton.   Both of St. Thomas' Parish.   p 12

9 January 1798.   Coleby SMITH and Sally Kendall, spinster.   Sur. Robert Kendall.   Wit. James Taylor.   p 45

26 August 1786.   Edward SMITH and Rose Warren.   Sur. Thomas Bell.   Wit. Francis Taylor.   p 18

26 February 1760.   George SMITH and Elizabeth Suggett.   This license found in an old fee book by J. W. Browning.   Both of St. Thomas' Parish.   p 1

19 December 1798.   George SMITH and Elizabeth Abell.   Sur. Caleb Abell. Wit. Charles Bell.   p 47

9 November 1775. James SMITH and Patty Cleveland. Found in Deed Book
17. Both in St. Thomas' Parish. Notation: by Banns. p 4

16 December 1807. James SMITH and Caty Smith. Sur. William Lindsay,
who makes oath Caty is over 21. p 72

14 September 1775. John SMITH and Jane Smith. Found in Deed Book 17.
Both of St. Thomas' Parish. p 4

24 March 1785. John SMITH and Elizabeth Warren, who writes her own
consent. Sur. Thomas Bell. Wit. Caleb Lindsay. p 15

20 April 1796. John SMITH and Sukey Smith, dau. Raife and Sukey Smith,
who consent. Sur. Absalom Tyler. p 39

22 October 1798. John SMITH and Nancy Sutton. Sur. William Sutton.
p 47

22 December 1800. Oswald SMITH and Joice Quisenberry, dau. William
Quisenberry, who consents. Sur. Caleb Lindsay. Wit. Aaron
Quisenberry. p 52

23 July 1804. Philip SMITH and Matilda Bickers, dau. Joseph Bickers, Sr.,
who consents and is surety. Wit. William Long, Edmund Hamilton and
Ellis Hamilton. Willis, son of Mathias Smith, who consents for him.
p 63

15 July 1777. Robert SMITH and Anne Conner. Found in Deed Book 17.
Notation: by Banns. Anne of St. Thomas' Parish; Robert of
Spotsylvania. p 5

27 June 1774. Samuel SMITH and Dorcas Douglass. Found in Deed Book 17.
Both of St. Thomas' Parish. p 3

4 July 1773. Stephen SMITH and Blessing Stevens. Found in Deed Book 17.
Both of St. Thomas' Parish. p 203

2 June 1783. William SMITH and Lucinde Smith, dau. Joseph Smith, who
consents. Sur. Rice Smith. Wit. Joseph Smith. William of Rocking-
ham County. p 12

16 November 1799. William SMITH and Mary C. Porter. Sur. Camp Porter.
Wit. Reynolds Chapman. Married by Rev. James Garnett. p 49

19 December 1805. William SMITH and Nancy Morris. Married by Rev.
George Bingham. p 67

8 September 1795. Caleb SMOOT and Martha McClamroch, who writes her
own consent. Sur. James Smoot. Wit. Nancy McClamroch. Married
10 September by Rev. George Eve. p 37

5 October 1805. Jenifer SMOOT and Rebecca Melone, dau. John Melone,
who consents. Sur. Michael Lower. Wit. William Melone. Married
by Rev. William Douglas, Methodist. p 67

9 June 1806. John SMOOT and Lucy Buckner Thornton, dau. George Thornton, who consents. Sur. Charles Thornton. Wit. William Buckner. John Smoot of Madison County. p 68

7 October 1799. John SMOUTS and Polly Fleek. Sur. John Fleek. Wit. Charles Bell. Married 8 October by Rev. Jacob Watts. p 49

22 August 1791. Joseph SNELL and Elizabeth Miller, dau. Robert Miller, who consents. Sur. Reuben Sanford. Wit. James Taylor, Jr. p 28

24 November 1806. Joseph SNELL and Elizabeth Clark Mansfield, dau. Robert and Mourning (Clark) Mansfield, who consent. Sur. Rowser Snell. Wit. Joseph Robertson. Married by Rev. William Douglass, Methodist. (Elizabeth Clark Mansfield b. 12 October 1788.) p 69

9 January 1797. Bird SNOW and Polly Mayhugh, dau. Polly Watson, who consents. Sur. Isaac Watson. Wit. Thomas Davis and John Snow. Married 12 January by Rev. George Bingham. p 42

9 January 1806. James SNOW and Jenny Harvey. Married by Rev. George Bingham. p 68

27 February 1800. John SNOW and Elizabeth Lower, dau. Peter Lower, who consents. Sur. Philip Boyer. Wit. Daniel Lower. Married 4 March by Rev. William Carpenter, Jr. John Snow of Stanardsville. p 51

10 June 1788. Robertson SPALDING and Fanny Jones. Sur. Elijah Jones. Wit. John Pendleton. Married 11 June by Rev. John Leland. p 22

7 November 1787. Edward SPENCER and Eleanor Woolfolk, dau. Christo Brockman (mother). John Oakes signs consent for Eleanor; no relationship stated. Sur. Joseph Woolfold. Wit. Samuel Brockman. p 20

4 November 1790. Francis SPENCER and Winifred George, spinster. Consent of Prettyman Merry for Winifred; no relationship stated. Sur. James Taylor. p 26

18 January 1791. Seth SPENCER and Ann Thornton, who writes her own consent. Sur. Abner Beckman. p 27

26 October 1799. Benjamin SPICER and Caty A. Snell, dau. Robert Snell, who' consents. Sur. James Cooper. Wit. Joseph Snell and Joseph Spicer. Married 9 January 1800 by Rev. Hamilton Goss. p 49

27 August 1792. Rawser SPICER and Nancy Wood, spinster, dau. Hanner Hensley and step-dau. of John Hensley, who consent. Sur. John Williams. p 30

10 May 1798. John SPRADLIN and Elizabeth Foster, age 18 years, dau. Lucy Foster, who consents. Sur. John Wormley. Wit. Henry West and Thomas Jameson. p 46

31 December 1804. Ebenezer SPRIGGS and Mima Sanford. Sur. Stewart Sanford, who makes oath Mima is over 21; no relationship stated. Married 3 January 1805 by Rev. James Garnett. p 65

29 May 1777. Daivd R. STAGE and Maryan Mooney. Found in Deed Book 17. Both of St. Thomas' Parish. Notation: by Banns. p 5

20 March 1786. Beverly STANTON and Jemimah Stanton, dau. Betty Stanton, who consents. Sur. Joseph Rogers. Wit. James Taylor. p 18

18 May 1791. Spencer STANTON and Sally Powell. Sur. Honorias Powell. Married 20 May by Rev. George Eve. p 28

27 November 1782. Achilles STAPP and Margaret Vawter, dau. Mary Vawter, who consents. Sur. Richard White. Wit. Thomas Stapp. Both of St. Thomas' Parish. p 11

4 January 1779. Thomas STAPP and Betsy Barbage. Both of St. Thomas' Parish. Sur. Joel Stodghill. p 8

24 November 1786. Samuel STEELE and Mary McQuiddy, widow. Sur. John Robinson. p 19

28 May 1799. Benjamin STEPHENS and Agnes Nelson, dau. James Nelson, who consents. Sur. Edmund Stephens. p 49

31 December 1796. Edmund STEPHENS and Agnes Robinson, dau. Agnes Robinson, who consents. Sur. James Nelson. p 42

26 December 1803. William STEPHENS and Elizabeth Nelson, dau. James Nelson. Sur. William Nelson. Wit. Goodrich Lightfoot Grasty. p 62

30 May 1809. Charles STEPHENSON and Susan Hancock. Sur. Willis Arnold, who makes oath Susan is over 21. Wit. Francis Day. Married 31 May by Rev. Robert Jones. p 75

12 January 1795. James STEVENS and Disey Gaines. Sur. Thomas Gaines. John Robinson consents for Disey; no relationship stated. p 36

22 November 1806. John STEVENS and Ann S. Stevens, dau. John Stevens, Jr., who is surety. p 69

10 October 1804. Merryman STEVENS and Ann Grigry, dau. John Grigry, who consents. Sur. William Merryman. Married 20 October by Frederick Kabler, Lutheran. p 64

29 June 1801. Waller STEVENS and Lucy Adams, dau. Thomas Adams, who consents and is surety. Wit. John F. Conway. p 54

9 February 1801. William STEVENS and Margaret Mills, dau. Nathaniel Mills. Sur. James Daniel. Wit. Charles Mills. p 53

23 December 1793. John STEVENSON and Milly Payne. Sur. Thomas Payne. Wit. James Taylor. p 34

15 January 1810. John STEWART and Catherine Reynolds, dau. William Reynolds, Sr., who consents. Sur. George Quisenberry. Wit. William Reynolds, Jr. p 77

2 November 1786. John STOCKDELL, Jr. and Sally Duvall. Sur. John Stockdell. Wit. Francis Taylor. p 19

23 January 1793. William STOCKDELL and Delphea Roszel, who writes her own consent. Sur. George Chapman. p 31

15 February 1797. William STOCKES and Lucy Silvey, spinster. Sur. Lewis Collins. Wit. Charles Bell. Married by Rev. Hamilton Goss. p 43

10 November 1786. Henry STONE and Nancy Golding, dau. William Golding, who consents. Sur. Jackey Golding. Wit. Elisha Estes. p 19

9 April 1799. John STONE and Elizabeth Burton, dau. James Burton, who consents. Sur. James Taylor. Wit. Capt. May Burton and Joseph Burton. Married 11 April by Rev. Jacob Watts. p 48

6 December 1803. John STONE and Judith Parrott, dau. William Parrott. Sur. William Parrott, Jr. Wit. James Rippeto and William Cave. Married 8 December by Rev. Jacob Watts. p 62

14 December 1802. John STOWERS and Sally Herndon, dau. James Gaines Herndon, who consents. Sur. William Dickerson. Wit. Edward Herndon and Michale Kinser. John, son of Mark Stowers, who consents for him. Married 19 December by Rev. Jacob Watts. p 58

4 July 1787. Lewis STOWERS and Joice Shiflett, dau. Elizabeth Shiflett, who consents. Sur. Mace Pickett. Wit. Lary Pickett. p 19

23 February 1810. Reuben STOWERS and Margaret Jackson, dau. Drury Jackson, who consents and is surety. Wit. W. White. Reuben, son of Mark Stowers, who consents for him. Married 1 March by Rev. Jacob Watts. p 77

21 July 1783. John STRAUGHAN and Mary Sanders, dau. Nathaniel Sanders, who consents. Sur. James Sanders. Wit. John Taylor. p 13

30 June 1807. George F. STROTHER and Sarah Green Williams, dau. James Williams, who consents. Sur. John Farish. Wit. William Williams. Married 1 July by Rev. William Mason, Sr. p 71

11 June 1775. William STROTHER and Anne Kavennaugh, widow. Found in Deed Book 17. Both of St. Thomas' Parish. Sur. William Cave. Wit. Francis Taylor. p 4

23 February 1801. John STROW and Catharine Walters, dau. George Walters. Married 24 February by Rev. Hamilton Goss. p 53

3 August 1796. Alexander STUART and Ann Reed, widow. Sur. Robert Stuart. p 40

14 August 1775. George STUBBLEFIELD and Sarah Morrison. Sur. Joseph Spencer. Wit. William Johnson. Consent of Richard and Catherine Reynolds, step-father and mother of Sarah. p 4

20 May 1791. George STUBBLEFIELD and Ann Hawkins. Sur. Joseph Bishop. p 28

20 December 1803. James STUBBLEFIELD and Polly Beckham. Jeremiah Beckham, who makes oath Polly is over 21; no relationship stated. Married 22 December by Rev. Nathaniel Sanders, Baptist. p 62

26 March 1800. Leonard STYERS and Elizabeth Wolf, dau. L. Wolf, who consents. Sur. George W. Switzler. Wit. John Miller and William W. Matthews. Married by Rev. Hamilton Goss. p 51

6 February 1789. Kenneth SUTHERLAND and Ruth Webster. Sur. Daniel Webster. Wit. Francis Taylor. p 23

6 April 1775. William SUTTON and Alice Brown. Found in Deed Book 17. Both of St. Thomas' Parish. Notation: by Banns. p 3

16 December 1791. Daniel SWENEY and Mary Griffeth, dau. David Griffin, who consents. Sur. Edmund Griffeth. Wit. James Taylor. Married 19 December by Rev. George Eve. p 29

17 February 1796. George SYLVA and Lucy Poe. Sur. Dennis Sha (?). p 39

5 April 1791. Hay TALIAFERRO and Lucy Mary Thruston, widow of William Plumer Thruston. Sur. Francis Dade. Wit. Lawrence Taliaferro. p 28

14 March 1797. Hay TALIAFERRO and Susannah Conway, dau. Catlett Conway, who consents. Sur. William Dade. Wit. James Taylor, Jr. p 43

12 May 1772. John TALIAFERRO and Amy (or Ann) Stockdell. This license found in an old fee book by J. W. Browning. Both in St. Thomas' Parish. p 2

31 October 1781. Nicholas TALIAFERRO and Anne Taliaferro, who writes . her own consent. Sur. Franics Taliaferro. Wit. Francis Taylor. Both of St. Thomas' Parish. p 10

28 November 1796. Henry TANDY, Jr. and Betsy Adams. Sur. Thomas Adams. Wit. James Taylor. (Elizabeth Adams was dau. of Thomas Adams and his wife Amey, Sister of Mary Adams who m. Roger Tandy. Henry Tandy, Jr. b. 15 September 1772, son of Henry and Ann Mills Tandy. 14 T 120). p 41

27 March 1809. Jackson TANDY and Sarah Mills, dau. Nathaniel Mills, Sr., who consents. Sur. Reubin Lindsay. Wit. Nathaniel Mills, Jr. (Jackson b. 31 August 1784, son of Henry Tandy and his wife Ann Mills. Henry's will Orange County Will Book 4 p. 331. Jackson and Sarah were first cousins. 14 T 120-121.) p 75

7 December 1795. Roger TANDY and Mary Adams. Sur. Thomas Adams. Wit. James Taylor. (Roger b. 3 September 1764, son of Henry and Ann Mills Tandy. Mary, dau. of Thomas and Amey Adams. 14 T 120.) p 38

26 December 1794. Thomas TATUM and Nancy Evins, widow. Sur. John Buchannon. Wit. James Taylor. p 36

16 July 1800. Edmund TAYLOR and Nancy Thornton, who writes her own consent. Sur. Willis Overton makes oath Nancy is of age. Wit. George Thornton and Reynolds Chapman. Groom is called Edward in consent. p 51

23 February 1795. Elisha TAYLOR and Dilla Walker. Sur. Jeremiah Sims. Married 26 February by Rev. George Eve. p 36

9 February 1788. Francis TAYLOR and Elizabeth Thompson. William Thompson and Joel Thompson consent for Elizabeth; no relationship stated. Sur. William Thompson. Married 21 February by Rev. George Eve. p 21

1 August 1787. George TAYLOR and Ann Stanton, dau. Charity Stanton, who consents. Sur. Francis Taylor. Wit. Dugustin (?) Anderson. Married 7 August by Rev. George Eve. p 20

20 December 1775. James TAYLOR and Deliah Stanton. Found in Deed Book 17. Both of St. Thomas' Parish. Notation: by Banns. p 5

26 December 1789. James TAYLOR and Sarah Hunt. Sur. George Brook.
Wit. James Taylor, Clerk. p 25

21 December 1795. James TAYLOR, Jr. and Frances Moore. Sur: Gabriel
Barbour. Wit. James Taylor. p 38

27 May 1799. James TAYLOR and Nanna Anderson, widow. Sur. Thomas
Roberts. This name may be Hanna. p 49

10 July 1801. James TAYLOR and Sally Wood, who writes her own consent.
Sur. Richard Wood. Wit. Reynolds Chapman. Married 12 July by Rev.
Hamilton Goss. p 54

25 September 1782. John TAYLOR and Elizabeth Kavenaugh, who writes her
own consent. Sur. John Price. Wit. William Strother. Both of
St. Thomas' Parish. p 11

21 December 1782. John TAYLOR and Mary Jarrell, dau. James and Sarah
Jarrell, who consent. Sur. John Farrell. Wit. James Quinn. John
son of Mary Taylor, who consents. Both of St. Thomas' Parish. p 11

28 September 1795. John TAYLOR and Elizabeth Pierson. Sur. Robert
Pierson. Wit. James Taylor, Jr. Married 8 October by Rev. George
Eve. p 37

30 November 1804. Jonathan TAYLOR and Elizzy Ann McDaniel, dau. Alexander McDaniel, who is surety. Married 6 December by Rev. Hamilton
Goss. p 64

2 June 1808. Larkin TAYLOR and Elizabeth Hume. Married by Rev. George
Bingham. p 73

11 February 1783. Reuben TAYLOR and Rebecca Moore. Both of St. Thomas'
Parish. Sur. James Taylor, Jr. p 12

31 July 1806. Robert TAYLOR, Jr. and Mary Conway Taylor, dau. Charles
Taylor, who consents. Sur. John F. Conway. Wit. Charles Taylor, Jr.
p 69

27 October 1809. Robert TAYLOR and Fanny King. Married by Rev.
Robert Jones. p 76

23 January 1800. Stanton TAYLOR and Elizabeth Stanton. Married by
Rev. George Bingham. p 50

30 January 1789. William TAYLOR and Elizabeth Walker, spinster. Sur.
Zachariah Taylor. Married 12 February by Rev. John Leland. p 23

24 November 1795. William TAYLOR and Susannah H. Gibson. Sur. James
Taylor. Merriman Marshall consents for Susannah. Married
26 November by Rev. Nathaniel Sanders. p 38

28 September 1805. William D. TAYLOR and Sarah G. Burnley. Sur. John Taylor. p 66

- - 1771. Zachariah TAYLOR and Alice Chew. This marriage found on a flyleaf of a memorandum book in Orange County Court House by J. W. Browning. p 17

19 December 1792. Zachary TAYLOR and Susanna Gerrell. Sur. Joell Cofer. p 31

29 January 1775. John TEMPLE and Mary Ann Canterbury. Found in Deed Book 17. Both of St. Thomas' Parish. Notation: by Banns. p 3

19 November 1809. Henry C. TERRELL and Delpha Smith. Sur. Samuel Teel, who makes oath Delpha is over 21. p 76

5 January 1789. Oliver TERRELL and Susanna Mallory, spinster. Sur. William Mallory. Wit. John Pendleton. p 23

5 September 1805. Reubin TERRELL and Susanna Morton. Sur. William Morton. Married 11 September by Rev. Nathaniel Sanders, Baptist. p 67

22 January 1798. Robert TERRELL and Ann Mallory, dau. Uriel Mallory and (Hannah Cave, in another hand). Robert, son of John Terrell (and Ann Towles, in another hand). Sur. Uriel Mallory. Wit. James Taylor, Jr. p 45

28 January 1793. William TERRELL, Jr. and Jane Morton. Sur. John Morton. p 31

24 November 1760. Edmund TERRILL and Peggy Willis. This license found in an old fee book by J. W. Browning. Both of St. Thomas' Parish. p 1

13 September 1810. Edmund TERRILL and Susannah Smith. Sur. Uriel Mallory, who makes oath Susanna is over 21. Edmund, son of Oliver Terrill, who consents for him. p 78

28 February 1803. Reubin TERRILL and Caty Gaines, dau. Robert Gaines, who consents. Sur. Benjamin Tinder. Married 3 March by Rev. Nathaniel Sanders, Baptist. p 60

23 November 1780. William TERRILL and Anne Daniel, spinster. Both of St. Thomas' Parish. Sur. James Taylor. p 9

14 May 1771. Zachariah TERRILL and Millie Walker. This marriage found on a flyleaf of an old fee book in Orange County Court House by J. W. Browning. p 17

26 November 1810. Emanuel TERRY and Nancy Oakes. Sur. Reubin Oakes, who makes oath Nancy is over 21; no relationship stated. Married by Rev. George Morris. p 79

22 December 1795. John TERRY and Lucy Oaks. Sur. James Mason. p 38

29 March 1808. Overton TERRY and Sarah Garnett. Sur. James Morton, who makes oath Overton is over 21. p 73

25 February 1802. Capt. Joseph THOMAS and Betsy Beazley, dau. Augustine who consents. Sur. Mark Hornsey. Wit. Mary Beazley. p 57

24 December 1787. Reuben THOMAS and Ann Spencer, dau. Joseph Spencer, who consents. Sur. James Brockman. p 20

9 April 1757. Robert THOMAS and Anne Moore. This license found in an old fee book by J. W. Browning. Both of St. Thomas' Parish. p 1

7 August 1793. Robert THOMAS and Polly Smith, dau. Joseph Smith, who consents. Sur. William Smith. Wit. James Taylor, Jr. p 33

5 April 1757. Roland THOMAS and Jane Thurston. This license found in an old fee book by J. W. Browning. Both of St. Thomas' Parish. p 1

3 April 1778. William THOMAS and Elizabeth Woolfolk, dau. Joseph Woolfolk, who consents. Sur. Robert Thomas. Wit. John Stevens. p 8

19 August 1784. David THOMPSON and Elizabeth Brockman, dau. Samuel Brockman, Jr., who consents. Sur. James Brockman. Both in St. Thomas' Parish. p 14

8 January 1798. Joel THOMPSON and Sarah Thompson, dau. Elizabeth Thompson, who consents. Sur. Walker Raines. Wit. Samuel Twyman. p 45

18 September 1809. John THOMPSON and Julia Pierce. Sur. Cypress Hensley, who makes oath Julia is over 21. Her name is Pierce one place and Price another place in the bond. Married 24 September by Rev. Jacob Watts. p 76

29 October 1801. Samuel THOMPSON and Sally Lindsay. Sur. Reuben Lindsay, who consents for Sally; no relationship stated. p 55

7 November 1809. Thomas THOMPSON and Frances Robinson, dau. Francis Robinson, who consents. Sur. Reubin Terrell. Wit. William Terrell. Married 9 November by Rev. Jeremiah Chandler. p 76

13 April 1785. William THOMPSON and Acquila Breeding. Sur. John Warren. Wit. William Boring. p 15

27 July 1795. William Theodocious THOMPSON and Jean McNeal. Sur. John Samuel. Wit. Pierce Sanford. Married 30 July by Rev. Nathaniel Sanders. p 37

18 November 1805. William THOMPSON, Jr. and Rebecca N. Ellis, dau. Thomas Ellis, who consents. Sur. John W. Sale. Wit. David Thompson, Mary Sale. William, son of William Thompson, Sr., who consents for him. p 67

20 November 1805. William THOMPSON and Catey Sinker. Sur. Brooks Sinker, who makes oath Catey is over 21. p 67

13 October 1778. Rhodes THOMSON and Sally Vivion. Found in Deed Book 17. Both in St. Thomas' Parish. Sur. Nathaniel Mills. Wit. Isaac Graves. Sally, dau. John Vivion, who consents. p 8

20 December 1791. Caleb THORNTON and Patsy Ford. Sur. James Sleet. Married 22 December by Rev. Nathaniel Sanders. p 29

22 December 1809. Charles THORNTON and Martha Ogg, dau. Alexander Ogg, Sr. Sur. John Ogg. Wit. Peter Ogg. Married 30 December by Rev. George Bingham. p 72

31 December 1800. George THORNTON and Nancy Webb, who writes her own consent. Sur. Reuben Webb. Wit. George Wells and George C. Taylor. p 53

22 July 1784. Jesse THORNTON and Ann Bohon, dau. Benjamin and Ann Bohon, who consent. Sur. George Waugh. Wit. John Boston. Both of St. Thomas' Parish. p 14

24 June 1799. Luke THORNTON and Sarah Sleet. Sur. James Sleet. p 49

18 January 1802. Peter THORNTON and Mary Miller, dau. Robert Miller, who consents. Sur. Thomas Miller. Wit. John Miller. p 56

26 December 1808. Thomas THORNTON and Elizabeth Wright, dau. William Wright, who consents and is surety. p 74

11 June 1770. William Plumer THRUSTON and Lucy Mary Taliaferro. This license found in an old fee book by J. W. Browning. Both of St. Thomas' Parish. p 203 says "Found in Deed Book 17." p 2

18 December 1797. Anthony TINDER and Lucy Robinson, dau. John Robinson, who consents. Sur. William Robinson. Wit. John Richards and Richard Robinson. Double Wedding: see Ike Richards. p 44

15 December 1802. Benjamin TINDER and Nancy Terrill, who writes her own consent: of full age. Sur. Reubin Terrill; no relationship stated. Wit. James Jones. p 58

29 January 1785. James TINDAR and Molly Shadrick, dau. Jobe Sandrick, who consents. Sur. John Shadrick. Wit. Thomas Shadrick. Married 3 February by Rev. Nathaniel Sanders. p 14

11 December 1786. Jesse TINDER and Aleapear Abell. Sur. Richard Abell. p 19

4 September 1796. Nathan TIRMAN and Tabitha Lowry. Married by Rev. George Bingham. p 41

11 April 1804. William TODD and Catherine Robinson Winslow, who writes her own consent. Sur. Joseph Chew. p 63

24 November 1785. George TOMLINSON and Elizabeth White, dau. Henry White, who consents. Sur. David Cave. Wit. Jeremiah White and Bellfield Cave. p 16

20 June 1780. John TOMLINSON and Mildred White, spinster. Both of St. Thomas' Parish. Sur. William White. p 9

23 September 1805. Solomon TROWER and Nancy Smith, dau. John Smith, who consents and is surety. p 67

6 April 1802. Thomas TRUE and Susanna Murphy. Sur. Nathaniel Middle-brook, who makes oath Susanna is over 21. p 57

29 December 1808. Thornton TUCKER and Betsy Biggers, dau. Mason Biggers, who consents. Sur. Hamlet Sanford. Wit. Henry Bowling. Married 30 December by Rev. Robert Jones. p 74

18 February 1806. William TULLOCH and Nancy Whitelaw, dau. Thomas Whitelaw, who consents. Sur. Nicholas Whitelaw. Wit. Charles Tooler. Married by Rev. William Douglass, Methodist. p 68

17 November 1802. Ezekiel TURNER and Sally Chissam, dau. Thomas Chissam, who consents. Sur. Joseph Croxton, who makes oath Ezekiel is over 21. p 58

12 April 1808. Fleming TURNER and Jane Clark, dau. John Clark, who consents. Sur. Thomas Wells, Jr. Wit. Edmund Clarke. p 73

2 November 1803. James TURNER and Sarah Loyd, dau. William Loyd, who consents and is surety. He also makes oath James is over 21. p 61

29 July 1790. John TURNER and Sarah Fitzgarrell. Sur. - Fitzgarrell. This bond is mutilated. p 26

3 October 1801. John TURNER and Elizabeth Brown. Sur. James White. p 54

31 January 1787. Thomas TURNER and Catey Brown. Sur. James Brown. p 19

2 February 1791. Francis TURNLEY and Susannah Watts. Sur. Robert Alcock. Wit. James Taylor. p 27

28 January 1790. Bononi TWENTYMAN and Elizabeth Nutty, widow. Sur. James Taylor. Wit. James Taylor, Clerk. p 25

16 February 1807. Anthony TWYMAN and Sarah Davis, dau. Isaac Davis, who consents and is surety. Wit. John Allen. Married by Rev. Jacob Watts. p 70

29 July 1809. John TWYMAN and Peggy Wayt, dau. William Wayt, who consents. Sur. Reubin Twyman. Wit. Samuel Twyman. Married by Rev. Jacob Watts. p 76

24 May 1802. Reubin TWYMAN and Drucilla Cowherd. Sur. Anthony Twyman. Married 2 June by Rev. William Calhoun. p 57

25 May 1796. Absalom TYLER and Frances Smith, dau. Jeremiah and Elizabeth Smith, who consent. Sur. John Smith. Wit. John Pendleton. p 40

21 January 1803. William TYLER and Mary Ann Herndon. Married by Rev. Robert Jones. p 59

4 January 1791. Gideon UNDERWOOD and Mary Dohoney. Sur. Rhodes Dohoney. p 27

29 August 1783. Vincent VASS and Elizabeth Manning, widow. Sur. Richard Dickenson. Both of St. Thomas' Parish. p 13

23 August 1798. Joseph VAUGHAN and Nancy Turner, dau. Ann Turner, who consents. Sur. James Turner. Wit. James Vaughan. p 46

16 January 1774. William VAWTER and Anne Ballard. Found in Deed Book 17. Notation: by Banns. Both of St. Thomas' Parish. p 2

19 June 1784. William VAWTER and Mary Rucker, "of lawful age," dau. Mary Rucker, who consents. Sur. James Stapp. Wit. Achilles Stapp. p 14

30 December 1808. John VEATCH and Nancy Cooper. Married by Rev. Robert Jones. p 74

5 January 1787. Lander VEATCH and Peggy Thorpe. Sur. James Taylor. p 19

4 September 1804. Isaac VERNON and Nancy Patterson. Married by Rev. George Bingham. p 65

30 April 1794. Nicholas VOSS and Mary Spotswood, dau. John Spotswood, who consents. Sur. William Banks. p 35

22 May 1797. James Gordon WADDELL and Lucy Gorden. Sur. Nathaniel Gorden. p 43

12 October 1773. Richard WAGGENER and Catey Gaines. Found in Deed Book 17. Both of St. Mary's Parish. p 203

23 July 1806. William G. WAGGONER and Lucinda Hansford. Married by Rev. James Garnett. p 68

14 October 1795. Benjamin WALKER and Polly Sims. Sur. William Sims, Jr. Wit. James Taylor. Married 19 November by Rev. George Eve. p 37

19 September 1797. Lewis WALKER and Polly Harris. Sur. Lindsay Harris. Wit. James Taylor. p 44

18 August 1783. Thomas WALKER and Miseniah Powell, dau. Mary Powell, who consents. Sur. Francis Powell. Wit. Elisha Sheerman and Maryana Powell. Married 19 August by Rev. George Eve, Baptist. p 13

24 November 1801. James WALLACE, Jr. and Elizabeth Day. Sur. Pierce Sanford. Married by Rev. Robert Jones. p 55

21 August 1807. John WALLIS and Nancy Randel, dau. William Randel, who consents and is surety; also makes oath John is over 21. Married by Rev. Robert Jones. p 71

30 September 1800. George WALTERS and Nancy Harvey. Sur. John Harvey, who makes oath Nancy is 21 years of age. p 52

27 April 1807. Isaac WALTERS and Elizabeth Pence, dau. John Pence, who is surety. Married 29 April by Rev. Robert Jones. p 70

6 May 1807. John WALTERS and Margaret Hambleton, widow. Sur. John Coleman. Wit. Reynolds Chapman. Married 8 May by Rev. Robert Jones. (Probably widow of Thomas Hambleton q. v. and dau. of John Coleman.) p 70

22 December 1799. Francis WALTON and ELizabeth Speers. Married by Rev. George Bingham. p 50

28 January 1808. John WALTON and Agnes Snow. Married by Rev. George Bingham. p 72

26 May 1775. John WARNER and Anne Walker. Found in Deed Book 17. Both of St. Thomas' Parish. Notation: by Banns. p 3

5 January 1802. Thomas WATKINS and Fanny Moseley. Sur. Leonard Moseley. Married by Rev. Robert Jones. p 56

11 October 1786. Abner WATSON and Elizabeth Dear, dau. Catherine Dear, who consents. Sur. Robert Lancaster. Wit. Thomas Dear. p 18

1 January 1801. Abner WATSON and Nancy Long. Sur. John Long. Wit. Reynolds Chapman. p 53

4 April 1799. Isaac WATSON and Susanna Robbards. Married by Rev. George Bingham. p 48

3 July 1800. James WATSON and Caty Lamb. Married by Rev. George Bingham. p 51

10 August 1789. Jesse WATSON and Milley Ballard. Philip Ballard consents for Milley; no relationship stated. Sur. Francis Collins. Wit. Charles Taylor. p 24

20 July 1785. Johnson WATTS and Suckey Davis. Sur. James Taylor. Wit. Elizabeth Davis and George Davis. Joseph Davis consents for Suckey (Susanna); no relationship stated. p 15

23 September 1773. Joseph William WATTS and Rachael Foster. Found in Deed Book 17. Both of St. Thomas' Parish. p 203

22 December 1785. Julias WATTS and Mary Eve, dau. Ann Eve, who consents. Sur. Prettyman Merry. Wit. Thomas Watts, and Prettyman Merry, Jr. p 16

14 May 1809. Thomas WATTS and Sarah Head. Married by Rev. George Bingham. p 75

4 June 1778. William WATTS and Elizabeth Beazley. Found in Deed Book 17. Both of St. Thomas' Parish. Sur. John Beazley. Elizabeth, dau. of James and Anne Beazley, who consent. p 8

19 March 1793. George WAUGH and Elizabeth Boston; both of age and each writes own consent. Sur. Pierce Sanford. p 32

11 November 1782. Richard WAUGH and Margaret Brown, widow. Both of St. Thomas' Parish. Sur. Andrew Shepherd. p 11

1 June 1807. James WEBB and Nancy Crash. Sur. Daniel Harner, who makes oath both are over 21. Wit. John Allen. p 71

12 October 1789. Jesse WEBB and Judah Jones. Sur. Thomas Jones. Wit. James Taylor. p 24

25 January 1790. Jesse Bennett WEBB and Sarah Mason. Sur. Charles Mason. p 25

15 January 1790. John WEBB, Jr. and Mildred Lantor, spinster. Sur. Jacob Lantor. Married 20 January by Rev. John Leland. p 25

28 June 1790. Vivion WEBB and Lucy Woodward, spinster. Sur. Henry Lee. p 26

8 July 1783. William Crittenden WEBB and Jane Buckner, "of lawful age". Sur. William Buckner. Both of St. Thomas' Parish. p 12

13 January 1785. William WEBB and Sarah Leathers, dau. John Leathers, who consents. Sur. John Atkins. In St. Thomas' Parish. p 14

23 January 1797. William WEBB, Jr. and Patsy Smith. Sur. William C. Webb. p 42

27 January 1798. William WEBB and Margaret Atkins, who writes her own consent. Sur. Caleb Webb. p 46

22 September 1806. William Bennett WEBB and Martha Lancaster, dau. John and Susanna Lancaster, who consent. Sur. James Mason. Wit. Benjamin Webb. Married by Rev. Nathaniel Sanders, Baptist. Double Wedding: See Mainyard Oakes. p 69

28 July 1788. Andrew WEBSTER and Ursilla Smither, who writes her own consent. Sur. James Gaines. p 22

18 June 1793. George WEBSTER and Mary Highlander, dau. George Highlander, who consents and is surety. Wit. William Eves. p 33

13 September 1810. Oliver WELCH and Betsy Mallory, dau. Uriel Mallory, Sr., who is surety. Wit. Uriel Mallory, Jr. and William Moore. Oliver, son of Nathaniel Welch. p 78

29 March 1773. Samuel WELCH and Jane Bruce. Found in Deed Book 17. Both of St. Thomas' Parish. p 203

5 December 1793. James WELLS and Fenetta Reynolds, dau. Joseph Reynolds, who consents. Sur. William Wise Reynolds. Wit. James Taylor. p 34

24 December 1805. Levi WELLS and Charlote Marshall. Married by Rev. George Bingham. p 67

28 January 1797. Martin WELLS and Sarah Marshall. Sur. Thomas Marshall. p 42

6 December 1793. Thomas WELLS and Mary Clark, dau. John Clark, who consents. Sur. John Clark, Jr. Wit. James Taylor. p 34

5 January 1790. William WELLS and Mary Harvey, spinster. Sur. Samuel Serivener. p 25

31 November 1801. William WELLS and Nancy Sams, dau. John Sams, who consents. Sur. Bledsoe Brockman. p 55

19 January 1790. Zecheus WHARTON and Sally Young, spinster. Sur. James Tinder. Wit. James Taylor and James Taylor, Jr. p 25

23 May 1803. Jesse WHEELER and Catey Cash. Sur. Joshua Tate, who makes oath both are over 21. Married 24 May by Rev. Robert Jones. p 60

26 November 1787. James WHITE and Lucy Wood, dau. James Wood, who consents. Sur. James Sebree. Wit. Richard Quinn. Married by Rev. George Eve. p 20

2 April 1792. Jesse WHITE and Elizabeth Martin. Sur. Robert Martin. Wit. James Taylor. p 32

28 July 1787. Joel WHITE and Frankey Rucker, dau. John Rucker, who consents. Sur. George Tomlinson. Wit. Galin White and Joel Rucker. p 15

8 August 1776. Jonathan WHITE and Nanney Martin. Found in Deed Book 17. Nanney of St. Thomas' Parish. Jonathan of Fredericksville Parish. Notation: by Banns. p 7

15 November 1786. Jonathan WHITE and Elizabeth Townsend. Sur. George Brooke. Married 16 November by Rev. George Eve. p 19

20 February 1783. Richard WHITE and Catey Olliver, dau. Tabitha Olliver, who consents. Sur. Belfield Cave. Wit. Joel Stodghill and Willis Olliver. Both of St. Thomas' Parish. p 12

8 February 1810. Richard WHITE and Anney Wayt, who writes her own consent. Sur. William Wayt. Wit. James Wayt. Married 11 February by Rev. Jacob Watts. p 77

27 March 1788. Thomas WHITE and Elizabeth Long. Sur. Zachary Burnley. Married 3 April by Rev. George Eve. p 21

4 June 1807. Thomas WHITE and Elizabeth Clarke, dau. Joseph Clark, who consents and is surety. Wit. John Allen. p 71

10 September 1782. William WHITE and Mary Brockman, dau. Samuel Brockman, who consents. Sur. John Henderson, Jr. Wit. Lewis Brockman, James Brockman and Mary Brockman. p 11

17 January 1809. Nicholas WHITELAW and Elizabeth Beazley, dau. James Beazley, Sr. Sur. Sanford Beazley. Wit. Robert Beazley. Married 19 January by Rev. Jacob Watts. p 74

25 November 1747. Thomas WIATT, Gent. and Suky Edmondson, dau. John Edmondson of Essex County, deceased. Prenuptial agreement between Thomas Wiatt of Essex County and Miss Sukey Edmondson. Orange County Deed Book 11. p 79 (1747)

21 March 1799. David WILLETT and Polly Baughon, dau. Thomas Baughon, who consents. Sur. Joseph Baughon. p 48

22 May 1807. Daniel WILLIAMS and Jane McCully. Sur. William Finnell, who makes oath Jane is over 21. Married 24 May by Rev. Robert Jones. p 71

5 May 1776. Francis WILLIAMS and Nanny Harvey. Found in Deed Book 17. Both in St. Thomas' Parish. Notation: by Banns. p 6

23 March 1795. Francis WILLIAMS and Sally Rogers. Sur. Samuel Ham. Wit. James Taylor. p 37

25 March 1786. Jacob WILLIAMS and Mary Delanay. Sur. John Atkins. p 18

3 June 1795. James WILLIAMS and Elizabeth Bruce. Sur. Thomas Farish. p 37

5 August 1800. James WILLIAMS and Sally Thompson, dau. John Thompson, who consents. Sur. Richard Cave. Wit. Capt. May Burton, Jr. and Reynolds Chapman. p 51

5 March 1778. John WILLIAMS and Elizabeth Rumsey. Found in Deed Book 17. Both of St. Thomas' Parish. Notation: by Banns. p 8

7 January 1788. Richard WILLIAMS and Nancy Rogers. Sur. James Early. Married by Rev. George Eve. p 21

30 December 1797. Richard WILLIAMS and Sarah Beazley, dau. Mildred Williams and stepdau. John Williams, who consent. Sur. James Beazley. Married 2 January 1798 by Rev. Hamilton Goss. p 45

29 February 1796. Thomas WILLIAMSON and Milley Bledsoe, dau. Aaron Bledsoe, who consents. Sur. Joseph Bledsoe. p 39

27 April 1772. John WILLIS and Sally Thomas. This license found in an old fee book by J. W. Browning. Both of St. Thomas' Parish. p 2

12 November 1804. John WILLIS and Nelly Conway Madison, dau. Ambrose Madison and granddau. Col. James and Eleanor (Conway) Madison. Sur. Paul Verdier. p 64

20 April 1781. Moses WILLIS and Elizabeth Thomas, dau. Joseph Thomas, Sr, who consents. Sur. Joseph Sleet. Wit. Joseph Boston and Fils Sleet. Married 25 April by Rev. Nathaniel Sanders. p 10

17 September 1776. Reuben WILLIS and Anne Garnett. Found in Deed Book 17. Anne of St. Mark's Parish. Reuben of St. Thomas' Parish. Notation: by Banns. p 7

8 February 1804. Valentine WINSLOW and Ann Beadles, dau. John Beadles, Sr. Sur. John Beadles, Jr. Wit. Sarah Winslow. Married 12 February by Rev. George Bingham. p 62

13 August 1773. Joseph WISDOM and Sarah Gardner. Found in Deed Book 17. Both of St. Thomas' Parish. p 203

20 December 1774. John WITHERSPOON and Mary Boston. Found in Deed Book 17. Both of St. Thomas' Parish. Notation: by Banns. p 3

19 October 1775. Ellet WOOD and Mary Connor. Found in Deed Book 17. Both in St. Thomas' Parish. Notation: by Banns. p 4

16 May 1780. Henry WOOD and Mary Weatherspoon, widow. Both of St. Thomas' Parish. Sur. James Taylor, Jr. p 9

1 May 1802. Hezekiah WOOD and Sally Bradley, dau. William Bradley, who consents. Married 2 May by Rev. Hamilton Goss. p 57

22 April 1793. Hopewell WOOD and Willy Terman. Sur. George Bringman. p 32

3 January 1807. James WOOD and Sarah White, dau. Jeremiah White. Sur. John Farneyhough, who makes oath Sarah is over 21. Wit. John Allen. Married 4 January by Rev. Jacob Watts. p 70

19 May 1806. Jesse WOOD and Nancy Page. Sur. Jonathan D. Goodall, who makes oath both are over 21. Married by Rev. William Douglass, Methodist. p 68

22 March 1781. Joseph WOOD and Margaret Bell, dau. Mary Bell, who consents. Sur. James Taylor. Wit. Alexander Dawney and Francis Madison. Both of St. Thomas' Parish. p 10

15 January 1807. Nicholas L. WOOD and Nancy Key. Married by Rev. William Douglass, Methodist. p 70

27 October 1806. Richard WOOD and Tabitha Cox, dau. Thomas Cox, who consents and is surety. Married by Rev. George Bingham. p 69

30 March 1792. Thomas WOOD and Rebecka Porter. Sarah Porter consents for Rebecka; no relationship stated. Sur. Pierce Sanford. Wit. Camp Porter. p 32

28 August 1777. Augustine WOOLFOLK and Frankie Thomas. Found in Deed Book 17. Both of St. Thomas' Parish. p 5

WRIGHT: see RIGHT

9 February 1808. Alexander WRIGHT and Betsy Jones. Benjamin Ficklen of Frederick County, guardian of Betsy, consents for her. Sur. Edward Holiday. Wit. Nancy Jones. Married 10 February by Rev. Nathaniel Sanders, Baptist. p 72

21 December 1799. Augustine WRIGHT and Mary Lindsay, who writes her own consent. Sur. Malachi Atkins. Wit. Reynolds Chapman, who makes oath both are over 21 years of age. p 50

5 June 1792. Benjamin WRIGHT and Ann Herndon. Sur. James Herndon. Wit. John Young. Edwin Young and Franky Young, step-father and mother of Benjamin Wright, consent for him. He is the son of Alexander Wright, deceased. Edwin Young married Frances Wright, widow, 19 December 1785. p 33

26 December 1791. Bledsoe WRIGHT and Sarah Beasley, dau. Augustine Beasley, who consents. Sur. Daniel Webster. Married 5 January 1792 by Rev. Nathaniel Sanders. p 29

27 August 1810. Dabney WRIGHT and Sally Bell. Brockman Bell, guardian of Sally, consents for her. Sur. Joseph Wright. p 78

5 November 1783. John WRIGHT and Margaret Jones. Sur. John Jones. Wit. Francis Taylor. Both in St. Thomas' Parish. p 13

25 September 1789. John WRIGHT and Susanna Grant Grasty, dau. Ann Grasty, who consents. Sur. William Edzard. Wit. James Taylor. Married by Rev. John Leland. Ministers' Returns dated 20 September 1788. p 24

23 January 1797. John WRIGHT and Elizabeth Sebree. Sur. Valentine Johnson. Wit. James Taylor, Jr. p 42

27 July 1801. John WRIGHT, Jr. and Catey Faulconer. Sur. John Faulconer. Married 4 August by Rev. Nathaniel Sanders. p 54

16 November 1801. John WRIGHT and Polly Shavers, widow. Sur. Edmund Clark. Married 17 November by Rev. Nathaniel Sanders, Baptist. p 55

25 August 1806. John L. WRIGHT and Nancy Wright, dau. John Wright, who consents and is surety. Married 28 August by Rev. Nathaniel Sanders, Baptist. p 69

26 November 1799. Larkin WRIGHT and Lucy James. Sur. George James. p 49

11 August 1787. William WRIGHT and Rachel Perry, dau. Pree (?) and Mary Perry, who consent. Sur. John Bledsoe. p 20

24 January 1803. John WYNE and Rachel Ahart. John Wyne, guardian of Rachel, consents for her. Sur. John Farguson. p 59

11 January 1809. William YAGER and Jane Chancellor, dau. John Chancellor, deceased, and Betsy Chancellor, who consents. Sur. John Chancellor, brother. Wit. James W. Hawkins. p 74

12 March 1812. Charles YATES and Betsy Loyd, dau. William Loyd, who is surety. Married 15 March by Rev. Jeremiah Chandler. This name is also written Yancy in the bond, but it is Yates in the Ministers' Returns. p 78

29 January 1798. James YATES and Sally Sanford. Sur. Abner Newman. Wit. James Sanford and Reuben Sanford. Wit. James Taylor. Sally writes her own consent dated 24 January with note "agreed to by Pierce Sanford." No relationship stated. p 48

27 April 1801. Armstead YORK and Joanna Hilman. Sur. Uriel Hilman, who makes oath Joanna is 21 years of age. Married 12 May by Rev. Nathaniel Sanders. p 53

19 December 1785. Edwin YOUNG and Frances Wright, widow. Sur. Benjamin Healey. p 16

11 February 1788. John YOUNG and Sarah Rogers, dau. Ann Rogers, who consents. Sur. Samuel Young. Married 14 February by Rev. George Eve. p 21

17 October 1795. John YOUNG and Frankey Grady, dau. Samuel Grady, who consents. Sur. William Grady, Jr. p 38

8 December 1803. John YOUNG and Mary Reynolds, dau. William and Nancy (Nixon) Reynolds; of age. Sur. George Quisenberry. Wit. William Reynolds, Jr. p 62

7 July 1800. Laurence YOUNG and Catharine Martin. Sur. John Martin. Wit. Charles Bell. p 51

29 November 1781. William YOUNG and Mildred Douglass. Both of St. Thomas' Parish. Sur. Edmund Massey. p 10

11 December 1775. Benjamin ZACHARY and Frankie White. Found in Deed Book 17. Notation: by Banns. Frankie of St. Thomas' Parish; Benjamin of Brumfield Parish. p 4

BURNLEY,
  Judith 1, 7
  Mary 78
  Sally 8
  Sarah G. 88
BURROUGHS,
  Mourning 37
BURRAS-BURRUS-BURROWS,
  Anne 3, 53
  Elizabeth 67
  Gestina 4
  Jane 70
  Mary 67
  Mourning 37
  Rosanna 75
  Suckey 62
  Susanna 24
BURTON,
  Elizabeth 84
  Fanny 14, 36
  Frankie 58
  Hannah 11
  Judith 9
  Lucy 20
  Mary P. 75
  Nancy 9
  Polly W. 13

CAMIKE,
  Polly 75
CAMPBELL,
  Peggy 3
  Virginia M. 58
CANTERBURY,
  Mary Ann 88
CARLETON,
  Martha 64
CARNES,
  Martha 64
CARTEE,
  Dorothy 56
CARTER,
  Catherine 68
  Judith 17
CARTEY,
  Betsy 35
CASH,
  Catey 96
CASSEN,
  Elizabeth 7
CATTERTON,
  Nancy 79
CAVE,
  Elizabeth 46, 48
  Frances 50
  Hannah 65
CHAMBERLANE,
  Alice 41
CHAMBERS,
  Caty 70
  Elizabeth 30
  Mary 1
  Rebecca 29
CHANCELLOR,
  Jane 99
  Penelope 74
CHANDLER,
  Jestin 80
CHAPMAN,
  Jenny 26
CHEW,
  Alice 88
  Milly 19
CHILES,
  Frances 33
  Frankey 3
  Jane 45
  Mary 20
  Sally 3
  Susanna 46
CHRISTY,
  Frances 16

CHRISTOPHER,
  Frances 11
CHISHAM-CHISHOLM,
  Betsy 29
  Catherine 33
  Sally 45
CHISSAM-CHISSOM-CHISM,
  Anne 24
  Mildred 66, 74
  Sally 91
CLARK,
  Ann 9, 65
  Elizabeth 65
  Jane 91
  Martha E. 18
  Mary 95
  Sally 79
  Tabitha 35
CLARKE,
  Elizabeth 96
CLEE,
  Elizabeth 53
CLEMENS-CLEMMONS,
  Mildred 62
  Polly 62
CLEVELAND,
  Patty 81
COFER,
  Judah 43
COFFERY,
  Anny 51
COLEMAN,
  Betsy 41
  Elizabeth 62
  Fanny 68
  Margaret 39
  Mary 45
  Milly 1
  Molly 61
  Nancy 29
  Nelly 1
  Sarah 19
COLLINS,
  Ann 66
  Anne 19
  Catey 33
  Elizabeth 37, 73
  Frances 27
  Jane 22
  Margaret 73
  Mary 51, 65
  Sally 75
CONNER-CONNOR,
  Anne 81
  Betsey 51
  Elizabeth 64
  Mary 44, 98
CONWAY,
  Elizabeth 30
  Susannah 86
COOK,
  Betsey 18
  Nancy 25
COOPER,
  Nancy 92
  Sally 50
COPE,
  Margaret 77
  Patty 75
COURSEY,
  Polly 66
COWHERD,
  Drucilla 92
  Sarah 9
COX,
  Ann 78
  Franky 36
  Sally W. 27
  Sarah 27
  Tabitha 98
CRAIG,
  Lidia 37

CRAWFORD,
  Jany 22
  Jemimah 75
CRASH,
  Nancy 94
CRESSOM,
  Betsy 46
CREW,
  Tabitha 51
CROW,
  Elizabeth 60
CUDDEN-CUDDING,
  Milly 4
  Peggy 65
CURTIS,
  Margaret 62

DADE,
  Sarah 22
DANIEL,
  Ann 88
  Frankey 42
  Jane 70
  Lucy 20
  Mary 13
  Nancy 22
DARNEL-DARNELL-DARNOLD,
  Anna 70
  Elizabeth 23
  Frances 46
  Lucy 74
  Susannah 46
DAVIS,
  Aggy 34
  Ann 5
  Betty 19
  Edna 49
  Elizabeth 9, 35
  Frances 26, 47
  Jerusha 23
  Lucy 15, 22, 36, 47
  Mary (2) 45, 67
  Milly 67
  Nancy 27
  Rachel 63
  Sally 36, 74
  Sarah 53, 92
  Suckey 94
  Susanna 38, 78, 94
DAWSON,
  Mary 17
  Nanny 61
  Polly Stev. 80
  Sally 29
DAY,
  Elizabeth 93
  Susanna 60
DEANE,
  Rebecca 49
DEAR-DEARE,
  Betty 36
  Catharine 46
  Elizabeth 94
  Franky 79
  Lucy 51
  Polly 9
DEBORD,
  Lucy 34
DEDMAN,
  Frances 55
  Mary 45
  Nancy 54
DEERING,
  Mary 75
  Sarah 49
  Susannah 31
DELANEY,
  Dise 38
  Lesza 71
  Mary 97
DODD,
  Anna 52

DOHONEY,
  Elizabeth 69
  Jane 5
  Peggy 19
  Mary 92
DOLLINS,
  Martha 22
  Sukey 61
DOUGLAS,
  Anne 6
  Dorcas 81
  Judith 11
  Mildred 100
DOVELL,
  Nancy 12
DUMSEY,
  Dysa 70
DUNCOME,
  Elizabeth 32
DURRETT,
  Betsey 45
  Diana 45
  Milly 70
  Nancy 13
DUVALL,
  Sally 84

EARLES,
  Polly 22
EARLY,
  Elizabeth 17, 24
  Frances 59
EASTIN-EASTON,
  Elizabeth 32
  Mary 24
  Nancy 24
EASTRIDGE,
  Theodosia 70
EATON,
  Elizabeth 27
EAVES,
  Sally 7
EDMONDSON,
  Sukey 96
EDWARDS,
  Frances 41
  Rachel 65
  Sally 53
EHART,
  Catherine 43
  Elizaberh 23
  Susanna 43
ELLIS,
  Rebecca N. 90
ELUCK,
  Polly 26
EMBRY,
  Judy 73
ESTES-ESTIS,
  Barbara 74
  Betsy 21
  Fanny 34
  Jenne 54
  Lucy 21, 40
  Mary Stansfield 40
  Milly 14
  Sally 39
EVE,
  Mary 94
EVINS,
  Nancy 86

FARGUSON,
  Elizabeth 74
FARMER,
  Frances 64
FARNEYHOUGH,
  Elizabeth 67
FAULCONER,
  Catey 99
  Elizabeth 58
  Frances 28

FAULCONER, (Continued)
  Jenny 28
  Lucy 63, 67
  Sally 37
FEARNEAUGH-FEARNEY,
  Anne 35
  Elizabeth 67
FEEN,
  Catharina 10
FELIX,
  Elizabeth 40
FENNELL,
  Lucy 25
FERRELL,
  Betsy 29
FINNELL,
  Alise 22
  Anna Rita 55
  Elizabeth 26
  Lucy 71
  Nancy 52
FINNY,
  Fanny 56
FITZJARRELL,
  Sarah 91
FITZHUGH,
  Alice 48
FLECK-FLEEK,
  Elizabeth 63
  Polly 82
FLOYD,
  Anne 70
FOORD-FORD,
  Ann 80
  Lucy 60
  Patsy 90
FOSTER,
  Caty 52
  Elizabeth 48, 83
  Mary 43, 72
  Milly 35
  Nancy 66
  Rachel 94
FREEMAN,
  Sally 48
FRANKLIN-FRANKLYN,
  Elizabeth 12
  Molly 12

GAAR-GAER,
  Margaret 41
  Sally 26
GAINES,
  Catey 93
  Caty 88
  Disey 83
  Elizabeth 5
  Jenny 32
  Mary 23, 41
  Urcilla 27
GARDNER,
  Sarah 98
GARNER,
  Jinnette 63
GARNETT,
  Anne 97
  Sarah 89
  Ursula 49
GARTON,
  Susannah 20
GEAR-GEER,
  Elizabeth 61
  Mary 50
GEORGE,
  Winifred 82
GERRELL,
  Susanna 88
GIBBS,
  Lini 26
GIBSON,
  Mary 56
  Susannah H. 87

GILLOCK,
  Sally 21
GOLDEN-GOLDING,
  Margaret 3
  Nancy 84
GOODALL,
  Betsy 72
  Sally 63
GOODRICH,
  Ann 15
GOODRIDGE,
  Betsy 15, 32, 66
GORDEN,
  Lucy 93
GORDON,
  Hannah 6
  Mary 36
  Priscilla 27
  Sarah 52
GRACE,
  Gracey 36
  Polly 10
GRADY,
  Anna 37
  Fanny 69
  Frankey 100
  Mary 9
  Sarah 28
GRASTY,
  Nanney 18
  Susanna Grant 99
GRAVES,
  Drucilla 11
  Elizabeth 18
  Joanna 63
  Lyddia 58
  Nancy 31
  Sally 44
  Sarah 37
  Susanna 61
GRESHAM,
  Sally 54
GRIFFITH,
  Nancy 85
  Sarah 27
GRIGRY,
  Ann 83
GRINNELS,
  Rebecca 60
GRYMES,
  Betsy Johnson 60
  Hannah 76
  Judith Robinson 21
  Mary L. 5
GRUNTER,
  Jemima 61

HACKLEY,
  Elizabeth 18
HALL,
  Nancy 18
HAM-HAMM,
  Judith 53
  Mary 74
  Sally 34
HAMBLETON,
  Margaret 93
  Polly 14
  Sarah 64
HANCOCK,
  Elender 39
  Polly 33
  Rebecca 7
  Sally 12
  Susan 83
HAMES,
  Sarah 79
HANSFORD,
  Lucinda 93
HARPER,
  Patsey 1

LUCAS, (Continued)
  Molly 59
  Rachel 57

MACKELANEY,
  Susannah 70
MADISON,
  Frances F. 74
  Nellie 44
  Nellie Conway 97
  Sarah 55
MAIDEN,
  Docia 38
  Elizabeth 42
MAJOR,
  Martha 36
MALLORY,
  Ann 88
  Betsy 95
  Cintha 23
  Elizabeth 66
  Frances 80
  Jestin 1
  Lucy 5
  Mary 16
  Nancy 5, 8
  Susanna 88
MALLY,
  Nancy 56
MANKSPOIL-MANSPOILE,
  Sarah 52
  Lucy 53
MANNING,
  Elizabeth 92
MANSFIELD,
  Elizabeth Clark 82
MARQUESS,
  Levina 10
  Marian 37
MARR,
  Ann 2
  Elizabeth 38
MARSHALL,
  Charlotte 95
  Jane 9
  Lucy Mary 23
  Polly 12
  Sarah 95
MARTIN,
  Betsy 21
  Catharine 100
  Elizabeth 96
  Jane 3
  Nanney 96
  Polly 47
  Sarah 46
MASON,
  Betsy 68
  Fanny 30
  Sarah 94
MASSEY,
  Mary 64
MAURY,
  Ann Tunstall 44
MAY,
  Milly 15
MAYHUGH,
  Polly 82
MAYS,
  Elizabeth 25
MAZE,
  Sarah 6
MC CAULEY,
  Polly 68
MC CLAMROCH,
  Martha 81
MC CULLY,
  Jane 97
MC DANIEL,
  Elzzy Ann 87
MC KINNEY,
  Elizabeth 36

MC KINNEY,
  Mary 55
  Sarah 11
MC MULLAN,
  Catherine 78
  Mary 69
MC NEAL-NEIL,
  Ann 36
  Elizabeth 67
  Frances 17
  Jean 90
  Martha 80
  Mary 83
MELONE,
  Rebecca 81
MERRY,
  Elizabeth 23
  Mary 76
MIDDLEBROOK,
  Elizabeth 65
MILBURN,
  Selah 8
MILLER,
  Ann 62
  Betsy 57
  Caty 29
  Elizabeth 55, 82
  Jane 14
  Mary 2, 90
  Sally 58
MILLS,
  Cynthia 15
  Elizabeth 26
  Fanny 52
  Frances 52
  Margaret 84
  Mary A. 28
  Sarah 86
MINOR,
  Ann 59
  Mary 62
  Sarah 35
  Susannah 63
MINTON,
  Fanny 7
MITCHELL,
  Elender 12
  Elizabeth 19, 45
MODISET,
  Ann 24
MONTACUE-MONTAGUE,
  Caty 37
  Hannah 36
  Nancy 53
  Polly 67
  Sally 4
MOONEY,
  Maryan 83
MOORE,
  Anne 31, 89
  Frances 87
  Mary 6
  Rebecca 87
MORGAN,
  Elizabeth 35
MORRIS,
  Nancy 81
  Patsey Oliver 63
  Polly 32
  Rebecca 1
  Sarah 54
MORRISON,
  Margaret 28
  Sarah 85
MORTON,
  Elizabeth 37
  Frances 56
  Jane 80, 88
  Sally 10
  Sarah 29
  Susanna 88

MOSELEY,
  Fanny 93
  Sarah 10
MOWBRY,
  Sarah 53
MULLICAN,
  Mary 79
MURPHY,
  Susanna 91

NAILEY,
  Frances 51
NEALE,
  Catey 65
  Polly 11
NELSON,
  Agnes 83
  Elizabeth 83
NEUMAN-NEWMAN,
  Burlinda 74
  Elizabeth 42
  Fanny 35
  Jane 11
  Mary 42
  Patsy 68
  Patty 42
  Polly 28
NICKINGS,
  Elizabeth 54
NIXON,
  Nancy 71
NORWELL,
  Esten 80
NOWELL,
  Zantipy 44
NUTTY,
  Elizabeth 92

OAKES-OAKS,
  Delphia 50
  Lucy 89
  Nancy 58, 88
OGG,
  Martha 90
  Polly 34
OLIVE,
  Jensey 39
OLIVER-OLLIVER,
  Catey 96
  Cency 5
  Elizabeth 43
  Milley 21
  Nancy 75
OSBORNE,
  Nancy 27
OVERTON,
  Mary 45

PAGE,
  Mary 32
  Nancy 98
PAIN,
  Elizabeth 46
PANNILL,
  Ann 50
  Elizabeth 24
  Sally 35
PARISH,
  Ruth 25
PARROTT,
  Judith 84
PARSONS,
  Nancy 14
PATTERSON,
  Mary 13
  Nancy 92
PAYNE,
  Betsy 52
  Dillah 18
  Elizabeth 30, 37
  Judith 27, 56
  Mary 56

PAYNE, (Continued)
 Milly 84
 Nancy 26
 Sally 18
PEARSON,
 Mary 31
 Peggy 2
 Tabitha 71
PENCE,
 Catherine 64
 Elizabeth 93
PENDLETON,
 Ann 22
PERESON,
 Frances 2
PERRY,
 Ann 10
 Rachel 99
 Sukey 43
PETROS,
 Nancy 39
PETTIS-PETTUS-PETTYS,
 Fanny 44
 Sally 47
PETTY,
 Frankey 10
 Lizey 18
 Patsey 80
 Rebecca 80
 Sally 49
 Sarah 41
PICKER,
 Catey 54
PICKETT,
 Esther 68
PIERCE,
 Julia 89
 Sarah 77
PIERSON,
 Elizabeth 87
PIGG,
 Anny 3
PIGLEN,
 Margaret 59
PINES,
 Winnefred 13
PITCHER,
 Susanna 10
PLUNKETT,
 Jenny 42
 Peggy 22
 Sarah 59
POE,
 Elizabeth 3
 Lucy 85
POLLARD,
 Betsy 55
 Nancy 24
POLLOCK,
 Elizabeth 74
 Peggy 6
PORTER,
 Ann 78
 Elizabeth 38
 Frances 73
 Lucy 7
 Maria 16
 Mary 79
 Mary C. 81
 Rebecka 98
POWELL,
 Betsy 7
 Elisha 78
 Frankey 7, 72
 Lucretia 78
 Miseniah 93
 Nutty 39
 Sally 69, 83
 Winney 18, 76
PRICE,
 Catey 60
 Elizabeth 31, 38

PRICE, (Continued)
 Mary Barber 22
 Milly 39
 Polly 35
PROCTOR,
 Betsey 68
 Sarah 36

QUISENBERRY,
 Amy 33
 Dolly 77
 Elizabeth 66, 67
 Jane 71
 Joice 41, 71, 81
 Lydia 26
 Mary 21
 Nancy 47
 Polly 8
 Sidnah 63
 Winefret 61

RAINS-RANES,
 Catherine 17
 Mildred 69
RANDALL-RANDEL,
 Elizabeth 75
 Nancy 93
RANSDELL,
 Betsy 76
 Molly 31
 Patsy 68
RAWSON,
 Sarah 72
RECTOR,
 Elizabeth 41
REDDISH,
 Lucy 2
REED,
 Anne 85
 Nancy 53
RENNOLDS,
 Peggy 61
REYNOLDS,
 Catherine 84
 Elizabeth 23, 53
 Fennetta 95
 Henrietta 70
 Lucy 8
 Margaret 70
 Mary 100
 Sarah 19
 Tabitha 16
RHOADS-RHODES,
 Frances 30
 Theodosia 72
RICE,
 Lucy 11
RICHARDS,
 Diannah 48
 Frances 39
 Patty 64
RIDDELL-RIDDLE,
 Fanny 20
 Joyce 72
 Winney 64
RIPPITO-RIPPETOE,
 Elizabeth 38
 Sarah W. 39
ROACH,
 Ann 71
ROBBARDS,
 Susanna 94
ROBINSON,
 Agnes 83
 Caty 48
 Elizabeth 29, 71
 Frances 89
 Keturah 6
 Lucy 73, 90
 Milly 17
 Siler 46
 Suckey 17

RODGERS,
 Annay 76
ROGERS,
 Elizabeth 50
 Nancy 97
 Polly 34
 Sally 97
 Sarah 100
ROSS,
 Margaret 40
 Mary 44
ROSZEL,
 Delphea 84
ROUTT,
 Winney 42
 Winney J. 56
ROW,
 Ann 13
 Cynthia 49
 Mary 13
 Milly 32
 Rachel 8
ROWZEE,
 Frances 39
RUCKER,
 Catey 15
 Frankey 96
 Mary 92
 Milley 41
 Polly 37
 Sarah 57
RUMSEY,
 Elizabeth 97
 Lianna 49
 Mary 25
 Nancy 59
 Peggy 71
RUSSELL,
 Patsy 14, 36

SAMPSON,
 Sally 76
SAMS,
 Nancy 95
SAMUEL,
 Polly 47
SANDAGE,
 Lucy 79
SANDERS-SAUNDERS,
 Elizabeth 77
 Joanna 32
 Mary 85
 Millicent 58
 Nancy 28, 29
 Sarah 78
SANFORD,
 Elizabeth 41
 Mima 83
 Nancy 41
 Peggy 3
 Sally 100
SAWYER,
 Mary 31
 Sarah 56
SCHENK,
 Anne T. 8
SCOTT,
 Anna 40
 Betty 76
 Elizabeth 41
 Lucy 21
 Mary 43
 Sally 40
SEAL,
 Elizabeth 72
SEBREE,
 Elizabeth 99
 Lucy (2) 58
SELF,
 Mary 30
SHADRACK-SHADRICK,
 Milly 77, 91

www.ingramcontent.com/pod-product-compliance
Lightning Source LLC
Chambersburg PA
CBHW021834020426
42334CB00014B/629